Nicholas of Lyra's

Apocalypse Commentary

T0126256

Commentary Series

General Editor

E. Ann Matter, University of Pennsylvania

Advisory Board

John C. Cavadini, University of Notre Dame
James J. O'Donnell, University of Pennsylvania
Thomas H. Seiler, Western Michigan University
Lesley J. Smith, Oxford University
Grover A. Zinn, Oberlin College

The Commentary Series is designed for classroom use. Its goal is to make available to teachers and students useful examples of the vast tradition of medieval commentary on sacred scripture. The series will include English translations of works written in a number of medieval languages and from various centuries and religious traditions. The series focuses on treatises which have relevance to many fields of Medieval Studies, including theories of allegory and literature, history of art, music and spirituality, and political thought. The translations strive for clear, straightforward English prose style. Notes are meant to provide sources and to gloss difficult passages rather than to give an exhaustive scholarly commentary on the treatise. The editions include short introductions which set the context and suggest the importance of each work.

Nicholas of Lyra's

Apocalypse Commentary

Translated with an Introduction and Notes by
Philip D. W. Krey

Published for TEAMS
(The Consortium for the Teaching
of the Middle Ages)

by

Medieval Institute Publications

WESTERN MICHIGAN UNIVERSITY

Kalamazoo Michigan — 1997

Library of Congress Cataloging-in-Publication Data

Nicholas, of Lyra, ca. 1270–1349.
　　[Apocalypse commentary. English]
　　Nicholas of Lyra's Apocalypse commentary / translated with an
introduction and notes by Philip D.W. Krey.
　　　　p.　cm. -- (Commentary series)
　　Includes bibliographical references.
　　ISBN 1-879288-78-8 (pbk. : alk. paper)
　　1. Bible. N.T. Revelation--Commentaries--Early works to 1800.
I. Krey, Philip D., 1950–　. II. Consortium for the Teaching of
the Middle Ages. III. Title. IV. Series.
BS2825.3.N4913　1997
228'.07--dc21　　　　　　　　　　　　　　　　　　96-52918
　　　　　　　　　　　　　　　　　　　　　　　　　　　CIP

Printed in the United States of America

Cover design by Linda K. Judy

Contents

Acknowledgements

I wish to express my thanks to my mentors and the scholars who have helped me in this project with advice and encouragement: Ann Matter for inviting me to do the translation for the series; my dear advisor and teacher in all things, Bernard McGinn, who introduced me to Nicholas of Lyra; my other mentors in medieval exegesis and apocalyptic, Robert Lerner and David Burr; and my co-worker in re-introducing Nicholas to the modern academic world, Lesley Smith. Thanks are due to James O'Donnell, whose National Endowment for the Humanities Seminar gave me time and space to make significant progress on the translations. I also wish to thank Tom Seiler and the editorial staff of TEAMS for their careful editing and my dearest friend and wife, René, who gave the proofs one final edit. I dedicate this book to René, my angel ascending from the rising of the sun (Rv. 7:3).

About the Translation

Nicholas of Lyra had a clear and plain style, but his sentences could be long, involved, and wooden. There are, however, interesting insights and revelations hidden within the commentary. I tried to put his style into idiomatic English, except when I thought the sense required staying close to the text. Since his commentary was a continuous one, punctuation was a challenge. He often put the biblical *lemmata* in the middle of a sentence and usually commented on a passage with short interpretations beginning with "That is," or "Because." I have chosen to punctuate the *lemmata* according to their biblical place in the verse and have generally treated each comment as a thought, whether it is a complete sentence or not. One can generally read the *lemmata* in a continuous fashion (sometimes Nicholas omits a verse or two), and one can fit the comments in between. Sometimes Nicholas will go over a portion of a chapter again, when he wishes to withdraw or amend an earlier comment. At these places I have repeated the appropriate verse number.

Consequently, one needs to be aware that Nicholas cannot be quickly checked on a particular verse or passage; he does not always follow his initial interpretation and will change his mind later in the commentary. For reasons of inclusive language and clarity (for good or for ill), I have used the New Revised Standard Version of the Bible (New York: The American Bible Society, 1989) for all passages in the Book of Revelation and the whole Bible which Nicholas interprets or cites. Where they differ from Nicholas's text, I have supplied my own translation.

I have used two editions for the translation of Nicholas's *Revelation Commentary*. My primary source was the *Biblia Sacra cum Glossa ordinaria . . . et Postilla Nicolai Lirani nec non additionibus Pauli Burgensis et Matthiae Thoringi replicis*, Johannes Meursius, 6 vols. (Antwerp, 1634). When the Antwerp edition was unclear, I used *Biblia Latina cum glossa ordinaria et expositione Nicolai de Lyra*, ed. Johannes Froben and Johann Petri (Basel, 1498).

Some Further Reading

For a comprehensive list of books and articles on Nicholas of Lyra, see my articles: "Nicholas of Lyra, Apocalypse Commentator, Historian and Critic," *Franciscan Studies* 52 (1992): 53–84 (which includes a discussion of the many medieval historians and texts that Nicholas cites and employs in the commentary); and "Many Readers but Few Followers: The Fate of Nicholas of Lyra's Apocalypse Commentary in the Hands of his Late Medieval Admirers," *Church History* 64 (June, 1995): 185–201.

The Cambridge History of the Bible, vol. 2: *The West from the Fathers to the Reformation*, ed. G. W. Lampe (Cambridge, 1969).

D. Burr, *Olivi's Peaceable Kingdom: A Reading of the Apocalypse Commentary* (Philadelphia, 1993), esp. Chapters 9–11.

H. De Lubac, *Exégèse médiéval: Les quatres sens de l'Ecriture*, 4 vols. (Paris, 1959–64).

R. E. Lerner, "The Medieval Return to the Thousand Year Sabbath," in *The Apocalypse in the Middle Ages*, ed. R. K. Emmerson and B. McGinn (Ithaca, 1992), pp. 51–71.

E. Ann Matter, *The Voice of My Beloved: The Song of Songs in Western Medieval Christianity* (Philadelphia, 1990).

B. McGinn, "Revelation," in *The Literary Guide to the Bible*, ed. R. Alter and F. Kermode (Cambridge, Mass.,

1987), pp. 523–41. The bibliography for this article includes a short list of modern commentaries on Revelation. There are many works by McGinn on the history of the interpretation of the Apocalypse; see especially *Antichrist: Two Thousand Years of the Human Fascination With Evil* (San Francisco, 1994) and *The Calabrian Abbot: Joachim of Fiore in the History of Western Thought* (New York, 1985).

A. J. Minnis, *Medieval Theory of Authorship: Scholastic Literary Attitudes in the Later Middle Ages*, 2nd ed. (Philadelphia, 1988).

B. Smalley, *The Study of the Bible in the Middle Ages*, 3rd ed. (Oxford, 1982).

Facsimile reprint of the Rusch 1480–81 edition of *Biblia Latina cum Glossa Ordinaria*, ed. K. Froehlich and M. Gibson (Turnhout, 1992).

Introduction:
Nicholas of Lyra's
Apocalypse Commentary (1329)

Surveys of the history of biblical exegesis and, in particular, the history of Apocalypse commentaries rarely fail to allude to Nicholas of Lyra O.F.M. (1270–1349) as the greatest biblical exegete of the fourteenth century. Late medieval and Reformation verses were written about him.[1] Nicholas was born in the town of Lyre, near Évreux in Normandy.[2] Since Évreux was a center of Jewish studies, he was able to cultivate his interest in Hebrew and to become thoroughly acquainted with the Talmud, Midrash, and the works of Rashi (Solomon ben Isaac, 1045–1105).[3] Lyra's attraction to Rashi's literal method would have a profound influence on his exegetical style.

At about thirty years of age, during the reign of Pope Boniface VIII and in a period dominated with high tensions between Philip the Fair and the papacy, Lyra entered the Franciscan cloister, founded in 1267, in Verneuil, about twenty kilometers from Lyre. How long Nicholas stayed at Verneuil is at present impossible to determine; however, given his intellectual gifts, the cloister undoubtedly sent him to study at the House of the Cordeliers in Paris, where he spent nearly all of his forty-eight years as a Franciscan.[4] In 1307, as a baccalaureate, he began lecturing on Peter Lombard's Sentences and in 1308/1309 became a regent master of theology in the theological faculty at the University of Paris.[5]

Lyra's Career as a Franciscan

Lyra's career as a Franciscan intertwined with the lengthy papal and Franciscan preoccupation with Franciscan apocalyptic thought and its relationship to the issue of "poor use" in the order. Documentary sources suffice to sketch Nicholas's successful career as a Franciscan administrator, teacher, and scholar who survived as a high official in a most traumatic era for the order.[6] During his life of approximately eighty years, Lyra, who claimed to have known a brother who became a Franciscan while St. Francis was still alive,[7] witnessed the order at the peak of its expansion and papal support and also torn apart and demoralized by controversies and persecutions.

No other issue in the stormy early history of the Franciscans troubled the order more than the question of "evangelical poverty" and its relationship to apocalyptic spirituality.[8] Only a brief historical sketch is necessary here to demonstrate how Francis, due to his perfect imitation of Christ, became an eschatological symbol both in heretical and in official Franciscan circles.[9] The identification of Francis's message with the Gospel and his imitation of Christ, even to being marked with the wounds of Christ, made it easy to grant him a role in speculations about "the last things in history" or eschatological thought. His imitation of the poverty of Jesus and the apostles and the identification of his rule commanding poverty in the order with the Gospel were central to the religious consciousness of the early Franciscans.[10]

Beginning in the 1240s, Franciscans interpreted the prophecies of Joachim of Fiore (1135–1202)—that two orders would soon appear which would fulfill the eschatological roles of Elijah and Moses—as predicting the mendicant orders. In the Franciscan interpretation, the mendicants were the "spiritual men" foretold by Joachim who would challenge the Antichrist and rule in the coming millennial state of the Church through perfect poverty. Between 1242 and 1249 Alexander Minorita, a German layman who became a Franciscan in the 1240s, reworked his earlier 1235 commentary on the Apocalypse to incorporate Franciscanized Joachite prophecies into it. Alexander's Apocalypse commentary became an important model for Lyra's *Postill.*[11]

The Franciscanization of Joachite ideas reached into the highest echelons of the order; adherents included the minister general, John of Parma (1247–54). John was a proponent of strict poverty and later served as a symbol for the Spiritual Franciscans.[12] In 1254, in Paris, the Franciscan Gerard of Borgo San Donnino initiated a crisis, called "the scandal of the Eternal Gospel," which forced John of Parma to resign. Gerard interpreted Joachim's three-age historical program to mean that St. Francis, "an angel of the sixth seal of the Apocalypse" (Rv 7:2), had ushered in an era that would succeed the present Church and the New Testament itself.[13] Joachim's writings would substitute for the Old and New Testaments themselves. In 1260 the authority and leadership of the Church would pass to the "bare-footed men" of poverty—that is, the Franciscans.[14] The secular masters, who resented the presence of the mendicants at the University and their papal privileges, rallied around Master William of St. Amour to launch a counter-offensive. Gerard was condemned in 1255 by a papal commission that was held at Anagni under Alexander IV, and he was imprisoned for life.[15]

In addition to Francis's Christ-like image and his apocalyptic role, he had prohibited that his Rule of Poverty ever be commented upon or amended. Therefore, according to the Franciscan Joachites, the "spiritual men" were to live in poverty as a special sign.[16] Unfortunately, Francis's prohibition caused special problems in the administration of the growing academic order, which found it increasingly difficult to remain poor. The majority of Franciscans tried to navigate between the demands of the Church for their services and obedience to the Rule but discovered that they were attacked on two fronts. As the successful order obtained well-built convents, large libraries, proctors, and agents, many in the rest of the Church argued that the doctrine of apostolic poverty was belied by the way in which the Franciscans increasingly lived.[17] On the other hand, the secular masters at the University of Paris questioned the Franciscan assumption that Jesus and the apostles had been absolutely poor.

There was no definitive statement on the doctrine of evangelical poverty until Bonaventure, John of Parma's successor, wrote his *Apologia Pauperum* in 1269. In this treatise on "poor use," Bonaventure resolved the issue for the majority of the order by distinguishing between "use" and "ownership." He insisted that Jesus and the apostles had practiced poverty, but he asserted that the order could maintain "simple use" of necessary goods while the Church actually owned them "in fact." In 1279 Pope Nicholas III gave official sanction to such an interpretation of the Rule and refined this "legal fiction" for the order in the bull, *Exiit qui seminat*, through which the papacy maintained legal ownership of the order's property and goods while the order merely used them, maintaining no rights to them.

Within the order itself dismay over any relaxation of the Rule of Poverty developed from the beginning, and a minority party called the Spirituals became a full-fledged protest movement in the 1280s. The Spirituals, largely followers of Peter John Olivi (ca. 1248–98), opposed the majority of Franciscans, the Conventuals, and insisted with Olivi upon the most stringent observance of the law of poverty in the everyday life of the order.[18] The Spirituals maintained that preoccupation with temporalities would interfere with spiritual things. The Conventuals, who represented the leadership of the order, agreed that Jesus and the apostles had practiced perfect poverty but held that the Rule could be interpreted to accommodate the needs of a large, successful academic and missionary order.

Olivi, himself a student of Bonaventure at Paris and a lecturer at Florence (1287–89) and Montpellier (1289–91), was not such a radical opponent of the Church's leadership as were to be his zealot followers.[19] Nevertheless, his writings provided a continuous source of controversy. His apocalyptic program in his *Commentary on the Apocalypse* (1297), which included prophecies assigning a negative role to the papacy regarding evangelical poverty, inspired Spiritual fears that the leadership of the order and the Church had become compromisers and enemies of the Rule of St. Francis. In his Apocalypse Commentary, Olivi made a distinction between the carnal church, which would be ruled by prelates and princes, and the spiritual church, which would be led in the future by those who practiced perfect poverty. In addition, he divided Church history into seven periods, following the pattern of the seven visions in the book of Revelation, and saw in his own era the overlapping of the Fifth Age of laxity and the Sixth Age of evangelical renewal inaugurated by St. Francis. This identification of the unique role of St. Francis in history and the emphasis on the imminent approach of a double Antichrist—the first, a papal antichrist who would attack the Franciscan Rule commanding poverty in the order, and the second Antichrist, who would persecute the faithful, namely those Franciscans who practiced perfect poverty—became the distinctive themes in the apocalyptic spirituality of Olivi's followers.[20]

Nicholas himself seems to have been moderate on the issue of evangelical poverty, but during his career as a Franciscan, papal policies regarding the Spirituals oscillated. Boniface VIII (1294–1304) condemned the Spirituals, but they enjoyed encouragement during the pontificate of Clement V (1304–14).[21] The struggle turned dramatic in 1316 with the elections of Michael of Cesena, an aggressive Conventual scholar from Paris, as minister general of the Franciscans and of the administrator, James Duèse, as Pope John XXII. Both the Spirituals and the Conventuals sought the support of the new pope to gain the advantage, but Michael Cesena was eager to enlist the pope's aid in crushing the Spirituals. With the pope's help, he accomplished this in short order.[22] After destroying the Spirituals, John XXII then moved to undercut the Conventual position on "poor use" as well, possibly as a result of his investigations into the orthodoxy of Olivi's Apocalypse Commentary between 1317 and 1326, when it was finally condemned. The relationship between Olivi's apocalyptic program and "poor use" made the entire fundamental Franciscan doctrine of "poor use" not only suspect but also dangerous in the pope's view.[23]

In 1318 a long papal investigation of Olivi's *Commentary on the Apocalypse* began resulting in a series of bulls which nearly destroyed the self conception of the Franciscan order.[24] When in 1322 John XXII threatened to overturn Nicholas III's ruling on poor use, the Franciscan Chapter General meeting in Perugia in May of that year responded with a long letter to the pope, requesting that the order's catholic and papally approved understanding of "poor use" not be altered.[25] This document was signed by forty-six theologians of the order in Paris and in England. A shorter declaration intended for the whole Church was also drafted. Among the signatories of both statements was Nicholas of Lyra.[26]

John responded with two dramatic bulls. The first, issued on December 8, 1322, rescinded the papal practice established by Nicholas III of owning the consumable goods of the Franciscans while the order merely used them. The second, issued on November 12, 1323, pronounced it a heresy to claim that Christ and the apostles did not have the right of possession and of use of those things for which there was biblical evidence.[27] In 1326, a few years before Nicholas made his final edition of the *Literal Apocalypse Commentary,* Olivi's Apocalypse Commentary was condemned.[28] The investigation into the relationship between evangelical poverty and Olivi's Apocalypse Commentary seems to have caused John to suspect the orthodox Franciscan self-understanding itself. The lengthy crisis in Franciscan self-consciousness seems also to have prompted two of the most promising Franciscan theologians at Paris, Peter Auriol and Nicholas of Lyra, to seek a different model for Apocalypse Commentary.

Nicholas was no stranger to controversy as he rose quickly to academic prominence at the University of Paris. His name appears for the first time as one of the Franciscan bachelors of theology present in the hearing in the affair of the Templars on October 26, 1307.[29] He was regent master at Paris from 1308 to 1309, preceded by Alexander of Alexandria and succeeded by James of Ascoli.[30] In 1309 Lyra also participated in an academic disputation, or *quodlibet*, at Paris including two questions against the Jews.[31] On April 11, 1309 (or 1310), his name appears with that of James of Ascoli as a Franciscan master in the ecclesiastical hearing at Paris for the Beguine and mystic, Marguerite Porete.[32]

Early in 1319, with the destruction of the Spirituals all but completed and with the Franciscan and papal investigations into Olivi's works, including his Apocalypse Commentary, intensifying, the Province of France elected Lyra provincial minister, responsible for the chapters of Paris, Champagne, Artois, Vermandois, Lorraine, Flanders, Normandy, Liége, and Reims.[33] The Spiritual party had been all but crushed by the alliance of the minister general and the pope, and the order itself, under Cesena's aggressive administration, investigated Olivi's works. At the Pentecost Chapter General in May of 1319 in Marseilles, the Franciscan leadership condemned Olivi's works, including his Apocalypse Commentary, and forbade at pain of excommunication their possession or study by any Franciscan.[34]

Not coincidentally, in 1319 a young Franciscan master at the University of Paris, a Conventual and favorite of John XXII, Peter Auriol (1280–1322), wrote his *Literal Compendium of the Whole of Sacred Scripture,* which was to become a standard textbook in the later Middle Ages.[35] His commentary on the Apocalypse, by far the longest commentary in the *Compendium*, broke with the standard Parisian Apocalypse commentary method and, understandably, with the Olivian method. Auriol's commentary will be examined later in this introduction as the primary model for Lyra's commentary of 1329. The controversies and condemnations of the Olivi commentary and the official lists of errors in them had an effect on the commentaries of these two Conventual Franciscan scholars.

Nicholas, himself an independent thinker, adeptly maintained working relationships with the Franciscan hierarchy, the papacy, and the French royalty. As his Commentary will demonstrate, at heart he was a Francophile.[36] In 1322, at the approximate age of 52, with the Franciscan self-understanding under siege, Lyra began his *magnum opus*, *The Literal Postill on the Whole Bible*, which he completed in 1332–33.[37] The *Postill* was a running commentary on the Old and New Testaments, intended primarily for theologians as a basis for dogmatics and as a reform of the over-allegorization of the Bible employed by Lyra's contemporaries. Nicholas tried to discover the intention of the human authors in the literal sense of the Bible by looking at the grammar, philology, historical context, and the place of the passage in the whole outline of the biblical book. After its completion, the *Literal Postill* was officially presented to Pope John XXII on March 30, 1331, and the Franciscan who presented it to him received one hundred gold florins in return.[38]

In 1325, during the long pause before the Franciscans reacted to John XXII's two bulls undermining the

Conventual self-understanding, Lyra was elected provincial minister of Burgundy, which comprised the chapters of Lyon, Dijon, Besançon, Lausanne, Vienne, and Auvergne. In 1325 Jeanne of Burgundy, the widow of Philip the Long, named Lyra as one of the executors of her will.[39]

During his six-year tenure as provincial minister of Burgundy, Lyra witnessed an escalation of the conflict between the papacy and the order, as the former allies against the Spirituals, John XXII and Michael of Cesena, now turned on one another. Michael of Cesena objected to papal policies questioning the self-understanding of the Conventual Franciscans, and the pope attempted to have him defeated as minister general at the Chapter General in May 1328. As provincial of Burgundy, Lyra was certainly present when the General Chapter re-elected Michael against the pope's wishes. Thereafter, John XXII simply deposed Michael, and the pope's appointee promptly purged all but fourteen of the thirty-four provincials who continued to support Michael.[40] Since Burgundy is not listed as one of those provinces whose minister was dismissed, it is highly probable that Lyra also attended the Chapter General of 1329 in Paris, which elected Guiral Ot as minister general.[41]

In 1330, at the age of about 60, Lyra attempted to retire from his administrative duties to write full-time at the House of the Cordeliers in Paris. His life's goal was to comment on the whole Bible in both a literal and a moral (mystical) fashion; his chief concern was that God would not grant him the length of years to finish.[42] Nevertheless, he had to postpone his retirement from public life when, after the Queen of Burgundy's death on January 21, 1330, Guiral Ot, the minister general, authorized Nicholas and the queen's confessor, William Vadenc, O.F.M., among others, to fulfill the terms of the will by founding a college for Burgundian students at the University of Paris.[43] On the nineteenth of December, 1333, Nicholas took part in the theological convocation at Vincennes summoned by Philip VI to condemn the position John XXII had taken on the Beatific Vision. His name was fifth on a list of masters, arranged according to prestige, who attended the conference.[44]

Writing his *Moral Commentary on the Whole Bible* occupied Lyra from 1333 to 1339. The intended audience for this work, shorter and less ambitious than the *Literal Postill*, was not theologians; rather, Lyra hoped to provide an economical and practical handbook for readers of the Bible and preachers. This *Postill* became a brief typological and allegorical series of notes on those passages of Scripture which could, according to Lyra, be properly given a "moral" interpretation. His responsibilities as an administrator did not seem to hinder the completion of his projects significantly, since he completed his two monumental works between 1322 and 1339. Both works are frequently found in the printed editions of the *Glossa ordinaria,* which contains Lyra's *Postillae* and the response to them by Paul of Burgos (ca. 1351–1435), a critic of Lyra's literal method.[45]

The Apocalypse Commentary of 1329

In a survey article, Bernard McGinn has aptly summarized Lyra's contribution to the apocalyptic exegetical tradition, calling him the popularizer of the "linear prophetic reading of Revelation" precisely "correlating symbols and past events."[46] The term "popularizer" is appropriate because Lyra was in no way the originator of the linear prophetic method of interpretation, nor was he the one to give it a definitive cast for the future. As noted earlier, Alexander Minorita, a thirteenth-century provincial Franciscan (d. 1271), probably created this commentary genre interpreting all of church history as prophesied in the consecutive visions of the apocalypse. And there were many variations of the genre in the later Middle Ages which differed from Nicholas's.

The genre is characterized by citing an image, symbol, or phrase from the Apocalypse and finding the appropriate fulfillment of its implications in an historical character or event. Although this correlation process was not new in the Apocalypse-commentary tradition, squeezing all of church history into the commentary and reading the images in the Apocalypse consecutively and not recapitulatively was new. Alexander discovered the historical fulfillment of the prophecy by searching available and relevant chronicles and annals and cited long passages to substantiate the correlation. In this way he told the progress of church history in great detail from the Incarnation to the coming of Antichrist and the Last Judgement.

Nicholas had other methods for approaching the Apocalypse available to him. One traditional method employed by earlier Franciscans was based on a dominant spiritualizing tradition from the time of St. Augustine. Tyconius, a fourth-century Donatist, and Augustine read Revelation in a nonhistorical and nonmillennial manner. In their reading the millennium of chapter 20 was the time of the church from Christ to Antichrist but was not to be understood literally as one thousand years. In this model, which dominated the western interpretation of the Apocalypse until the twelfth century, the symbols and characters of the Apocalypse portray enduring problems of church history such as conflicts between heretics and the orthodox or between hypocrites and saints. Antichrist was coming, but one cannot know when. The idea transmitted by Tyconius—that each vision of the Apocalypse recapitulates separately these same recurring problems of church history—was an interpretive key to many commentaries in this tradition, such as that of the Venerable Bede.

A second model, with variations, was available to Nicholas via Franciscans who followed the interpretation of the Calabrian abbot Joachim of Fiore (d. 1202). Joachim still thought that each vision separately recapitulated all of church history, but he thoroughly historicized them: he believed the visions predicted specific, identifiable events in church history rather than reiterating timeless general problems. Furthermore, he interpreted Rv 20 with a vibrant millenarianism. In this model each of the seven visions in the Apocalypse provided a tour through the concrete events of church history, and consequently the figure of Antichrist was identified as playing varied roles in different symbols of the Apocalypse.

As noted earlier, Joachim's prophecies and his theology of history held special fascination for the mendicants and for many Franciscan commentators who, like Bonaventure, were sure the endtime prophecies included St. Francis.[47] Joachim's most famous disciple, the Apocalypse commentator Peter John Olivi, raised the

Franciscan fascination with the Apocalypse to a new degree. While earlier mendicant commentators used the Apocalypse to criticize clerical opponents and other adversaries, Olivi prophesied that the pope himself would become the enemy of evangelical poverty, and, as was discussed above, more than any other Franciscan he gave St. Francis and poverty eschatological roles that rivalled the significance of the papacy. Pope John XXII condemned Olivi's *Commentary on Revelation* (1298) posthumously in 1326. Nicholas revised and completed his *Commentary on the Apocalypse* in 1329.

There is little doubt that Lyra had two commentaries on his writing table as he wrote: Alexander's, as well as that of Nicholas's junior colleague, Peter Auriol, whom Alexander also influenced. Peter Auriol (1280–1322), soon to become Archbishop of Aix (1321) and an ally of Pope John XXII against the Spirituals, modeled his Apocalypse Commentary in his *Literal Compendium of the Whole of Sacred Scripture* (1319) on Alexander's, because the method seems to have provided Peter with a thoroughgoing historical approach that could avoid the anti-papal and reforming tendencies and, most importantly, the three-age Joachimist outline of history that the Franciscan Spirituals had used.

There is a readily discernible progression of influence from the method of Alexander to that of Peter and then to that of Nicholas. Peter Auriol only infrequently varies the precise correlations made by Alexander between historical personages and the Apocalypse's symbols, although his commentary is shorter, better crafted, and tells the story by merely referring to histories without directly quoting them. Lyra's *Postill* on the Apocalypse is a critical response to his more proximate model, Peter, and only secondarily to Alexander, and therefore it is important to summarize Peter's program.

Like Alexander, Peter seeks to find rhyme or reason in the contingencies of church history by selecting the key personages and events determined from the end of history. In John's seven visions he sees prophesied the oscillating periods of tribulations and triumphs in church history, progressing in a linear fashion until there will be an ultimate victory of the church triumphant beyond time. Peter finds purpose in the apparent randomness of history by organizing his story from the goal toward which history points, namely, the complete freedom of the Church from secular powers and the absolute authority of the papacy in the Church. The method finds the historical signs of progress and setbacks for the Church using the Apocalypse as a map. Using the traditional method of seeing seven visions in the Apocalypse, Peter interprets them as prophesying six consecutive epochs in history. Peter's interpretation is non-millenarian, but there is advancement in the Church's gains through history.

A summary of his account would look like the following: The early Christian mission triumphs over the Roman persecutions, blossoms in the Constantinian era because it is granted power to rule in the Donation of Constantine, and is challenged by heresies and Julian's apostasy. Order and religion for the Empire are codified in the Justinian Digest so that heresies can be defeated in an orderly fashion. The pagan invasions challenge the new order, but once again angels rise to the occasion with the Carolingians establishing a new peace for the Church, culminating in Boniface's successful mission to the

Germans. Interest is not only devoted to the West. The challenge of the Persian Chosroes to the Eastern Empire and the angel Heraclius, who defeats him, attracts considerable attention; Chosroes is none other than the dragon of Rv 13. Due in part to heresy, the Empire is translated from the East to the West under Charlemagne.

Nevertheless, as with Alexander, for Auriol the Holy Roman Empire changes roles from a positive force to a negative one as Gregory VII must free the Church from nearly three centuries of simony and lay-investiture. The Church at liberty can properly conduct its mission. In the Concordat at Worms in 1122 Pope Calixtus binds the dragon, the Empire. However, no challenge to the Christian mission is more critical than that of Islam (Muhammad is the beast from the earth), and no triumph is sweeter than the First Crusade, when saints from so many countries responded to the call and established the Latin Kingdom in the Holy Land (Alexius, Godfrey, Ademar, and Baldwin are all protagonists). The Islamic rulers of the Turks and Egypt are assigned negative images, as is Frederick II.

Central to Auriol's theology of history is the determination that the new twelfth-century orders and especially the thirteenth-century mendicant orders are harbingers of the ultimate ahistorical triumph. The world is actually renewed in the preaching of Dominic and Francis. The thirteenth-century Alexander is much more optimistic about the eschatological role of the mendicants than is Auriol. Alexander interprets the elaborate description of the city of Jerusalem in Rv 21 as prophecy of the design and mission of the mendicant orders. Innocent III is naturally given pride of place as the pope who welcomes these orders into the Church.

Peter Auriol does not end his narration of history here. A brief summary of his account of history to his own time is in order before Lyra's response is summarized. The dragon of simony that devastates the Church will be bound for one thousand years. This thousand years is not computed from the time of Calixtus, nor from the Incarnation, but from the time of Constantine and Sylvester under whom priests began to rule. In Rv 20:4 the Premonstratensians and the Cistercians are foreseen and monasteries are spread far and wide, especially through St. Bernard. The fall of Jerusalem in 1237 is narrated, as well as the regaining of Damietta and Acre. In 1229 the conflict between Papacy and Empire is rekindled between Innocent IV and Frederick II, the consequences of which will last until the coming of Antichrist. The first resurrection of Rv 20:4 refers to the foundation of the Franciscans and Dominicans. Auriol ends this chapter by repeating his computation of the thousand years to the release of Antichrist from the time of Constantine. Since the end would be close to Peter's own time, he claims that only the Holy Spirit really knows when Antichrist will return.

Nicholas's Program

Lyra's historiographical revision of the prophetic-linear genre can be attributed in part to "hard-nosed" scholarship, in part to personal theological opinions, and in part to the low morale of the Franciscan order when he wrote his *Literal Postill* in 1329. The conflicts among the

Franciscans over the role of poverty in obedience to Francis's rule and the propriety of communal wealth due to institutional success had turned particularly ugly and dangerous after Pope John XXII condemned, in a series of bulls (1322–29), the delicate distinction between "use and ownership."

Lyra had a reputation as the moderate and rational doctor, and his commentary is littered with phrases like, "It is more rational to say . . ." or "Some expositors say . . . , but it would be better to say . . ." or "Some say . . . , but with better judgement it seems better to say. . . ." Lyra at times seems far more interested in discussing the mistakes in the methodologies of Alexander and Peter Auriol than in presenting an outline of history of his own. Lyra corrects the interpretations of his models, thereby allowing a chastened view of the Christian mission to emerge that is dominated by christology, trinitarianism, eucharistic piety, and ecclesiology. He is not as triumphalist about the Papal-Church, the crusades, and the promise of the mendicants as are Alexander and Peter Auriol. In his opinion, the facts in the histories do not substantiate such claims. The amount of material in the Apocalypse that Lyra actually interprets in a linear-historical fashion is small compared to that interpreted in his sources, Alexander and Peter.

Lyra relentlessly uses two means to correct his sources. The first means is the use of his famous *double literal sense* which serves as his key to interpret Old Testament passages. This hermeneutical tool allows the exegete to draw two interpretations from a prophetic passage: one meaning for the prophet's own time and another for the future that it promises. The literal historical sense is concerned with the story line and a literal prophetic sense is concerned with the story's theological significance.[48] According to Lyra, this allows for a "literal" Christological interpretation of an Old Testament text without doing violence to the literal meaning for its own time. Expositors fail, according to Lyra, when they do not recognize that certain symbols, due to their context in the passage, can only apply to John's own time. At crucial points in the commentary Lyra appeals to this principle to defuse what he thinks to be overstated or overly enthusiastic interpretations; however, Nicholas does not always use the double nature of his interpretive method. In spite of the fact that he considers the Apocalypse a prophetic work, he frequently allows only the one contemporaneous meaning.

Second, Lyra carefully reads the chronicles and annals available to him and critiques his sources' interpretations of the texts.[49] Alexander of Bremen used Frutolf-Ekkehard as his primary source. Other annals and Jacques de Vitry's *Historia Orientalis* are also cited but less frequently. As was noted before, Peter Auriol's sources are not easily identified. It is doubtful whether Peter or Nicholas had Frutolf-Ekkehard at their disposal. Lyra cites his historical sources, often by book and chapter. The chronicles and histories he regularly cites are Eusebius's *Ecclesiastical History*, Jerome's *Lives of Famous Men,* Hugh of Fleury's *Historia Ecclesiastica* (1109), Sigebert of Gembloux's (1030–1112) *Chronicles,* the *Legenda Exaltationis Sanctae Crucis*, Peter Comestor's († ca. 1179) *Historia Scholastica*, the *Historia Hierosolymitana* of Ekkehard, William of Tyre's (ca. 1130–86) *Historia rerum in partibus transmarinis gestarum*, Vincent of Beauvais's (ca. 1190–ca. 1264) *Speculum Historiale*, James of Vitry's (ca. 1160–1240) *Historia Orientalis*, and individual reports of travelling friars and one bishop whom he knew. As he makes a revision, Lyra will regularly insist that the context of what precedes or follows the interpreted passage of Revelation does not match the historical account as recorded. He will suggest an unnamed possibility, or he will reject the correlation of his sources for a christological, trinitarian, sacramental, or ecclesial solution. It is interesting to note that in his literal commentary he rarely chooses a moral interpretation.

After Lyra's revisions, church history looked different. It still moved forward with development and change as in Peter's account; one can even detect the distinct periods marked off by key figures whom Peter identified. Nevertheless, the heroes and villains of history became harder to identify. Although, when considered as a whole his biases are clear, he hides them behind the facts narrated in the histories. The Emperor Constantine, who ended the era of persecution and showered the Church with resources, is an undisputed protagonist. Pope Sylvester stands alongside Constantine in a similar, but not superior, role. No one in Lyra's account receives as many accolades as Charlemagne. The only criticism Lyra can muster against him is that his crusades against the Muslims did not endure. Lyra does not repeat Peter's protests that Charlemagne and his successors overstepped their bounds. Gregory VII and Henry IV were, unfortunately, in conflict, but Lyra refuses to assign blame. If he were forced to choose the instigator, it would not be Henry. Nicholas respected the ability of secular rulers to serve as protectors of the Church, even though he thought they basically should stick to temporal affairs.

The ecclesial triumphalism as expressed in the crusades, the lack of any reforming rhetoric for the Church, and the bias for the papacy in the Investiture controversies are themes in Auriol that fall away in Lyra. The crusades were temporary accomplishments marred by human greed and sinfulness and should not be overblown. Although the first crusade achieved a modest success, its accomplishments were in part due to the divisions among the Muslims and did not endure; everything gained was eventually lost. This brings Nicholas to the end of chapter 16 in the Apocalypse.

Nicholas's narration of church history goes only to the twelfth century. He insists that chapters 17 to the middle of 20 of the Apocalypse are about current and future events, and, since he does not have the prophetic gifts to assess the contemporary situation or the future, he avoids interpreting them. Nevertheless, he is willing to criticize in great detail Peter's and Alexander's attempts to interpret those chapters. Chapters 17 to the middle of 20, thus, are not Lyra's constructive commentary but are a summary and critical appraisal of his models. In Rv 20 he offers a thoroughgoing critique. This style makes for very difficult reading and has caused Lyra to be regularly misunderstood in the tradition, such that Peter Auriol's views were often assumed to be Lyra's own.

In chapter 21 the eschatological role of Francis and the mendicants provides another point of difference between Auriol and Lyra. For Auriol, the mendicants renew the world, not in a way that supersedes the institutional church but as a function of its advancement.

It is, after all, Pope Innocent III who welcomes the mendicants into the Church's mission. Lyra is more ambivalent about the role of the mendicants. If chapters 17 to 20 could be viewed as complete, he argues, the angel with the key and the dragon could be interpreted as Innocent III accepting the mendicants into the church. The mendicants bind heresies with their preaching and thus renew the world. But the fact of the matter for Lyra is that one must view these chapters as incomplete.

If this point is too subtle, Lyra makes his ambivalence about the mendicants clearer when in his commentary on chapter 21 he criticizes Alexander for interpreting Dominic and Francis and their orders as the foundations of John's vision of Jerusalem. This identification can only be understood mystically, Lyra argues, not literally. First, he points out that the angel who shows John Jerusalem cannot be Innocent III because Innocent lived more than one thousand years after John. Second, after describing the beauty and holiness of the heavenly city, he demonstrates his now familiar realism and reasonableness. Not all mendicants are pure; nor do all who enter well persevere in the good, but many are apostates and scoundrels. He concludes by quoting Augustine's saying that just as he did not find any better than those who progressed in monasteries, so also he found none worse than those who were failures in monasteries. There is a chastened tone in Lyra's commentary that one does not find in Auriol.

Lyra, therefore, does not accept the apocalyptic role that the Franciscans traditionally assigned to St. Francis. The Franciscan mission did not look too promising in his context, and seemed more in need of reform than eschatological propaganda. A chastened eschatology turns

Lyra away from images of the mendicants as the foundation of the new Jerusalem to an equally Franciscan focus on christology, sacramental piety, trinitarianism, and a balanced ecclesiology. Lyra's account was a modified Augustinian revision of the church history his models had written. He was thoroughly loyal to the Church, but he refused to follow his models and identify those rulers who came into conflict with the papacy as the antagonists in the Apocalypse. Although he was a Franciscan administrator (perhaps *because* he was an administrator), he did not see the Apocalypse as a tool of propaganda for the order, as did Alexander and Peter Auriol. Lyra's account is hopeful for the future of the Church but imbued with a profound sense of the ambiguities of history. The pattern loses its clarity for him in the narrative after chapter 16; tragic and even ironic themes invade the Church's heroic march through the complexities of history detailed in the narratives of his models. The key to the Book of Revelation and all of history is the incarnation and the death and resurrection of Christ.

Notes

1. Hätte Lyra nicht über die Bibel geschrieben /wäre mancher Doctor ein Esel geblieben; Si Lyra non Lyrasset / Ecclesia Dei non saltasset; Si Lyra non Lyrasset / Lutherus non saltasset. *Dictionnaire de la Théologie Catholique*, s.v. "Lyre (Nicholas de)" by F. Vernet. The verses may be translated, "If Lyra had not commented on the Bible, many a professor would have remained a jackass; If Lyra had not lyred, the Church of God would not have danced; If Lyra had not lyred, Luther would not have danced."

2. Henri Labrosse and C. V. Langlois produced significant manuscript and biographical studies outlining the chronology of Lyra's life and works, using Nicholas's own dating. These scholars charted the veritable sea of extant manuscripts. Henri Labrosse, "Sources de la biographie de Nicolas de Lyre," *Études franciscaines* [henceforth *EF*] 16 (1906): 383–404; idem, "Biographie de Nicolas de Lyre," *EF* 17 (1907): 489–505, 593–608; idem, "Oeuvres de Nicolas de Lyre: sources bibliographiques," *EF* 19 (1908): 41–53, 153–76, 368–80, and *EF* 35 (1923): 171–87, 400–32; Charles Langlois, "Nicolas de Lyre, Frère Mineur," *Histoires Littéraire de la France* 36 (1927): 356–57. More recently, Henri de Lubac devoted a lengthy section to Nicholas in the second part of his famous *Exégèse Médiévale*: Henri de Lubac, *Exégèse Médiévale: Les quatre sens de l'Ecriture*, 4 vols. (Paris: Aubier, 1959–64); see esp. 2, Pt. 2: 344–67. See also Edward A. Gosselin, "Bibliographical Survey: A Listing of the Printed Editions of Nicolaus de Lyra," *Traditio* 26 (1970): 399–426 (esp. Gosselin's lengthy bibliographical note on p. 399). For more bibliography see my article, "Nicholas of Lyra, Apocalypse Commentator, Historian and Critic," *Franciscan Studies* 52 (1992): 53–84.

3. Herman Hailperin provided a glowing and informative analysis of Nicholas's use of the great medieval Jewish commentator, Rashi: Herman Hailperin, *Rashi and the Christian Scholars* (Pittsburg: University of Pittsburgh Press, 1963); Jeremy Cohen contributed an important response to Hailperin's work in his book, *The Friars and the Jews: The Evolution of Medieval Anti-Judaism* (Ithaca: Cornell University Press, 1982).

4. The date of Lyra's entry into the order has been determined from a late sixteenth-century record of the epitaph on his tomb in the chapter hall of the House of the Cordeliers in Paris. (Labrosse, *EF* 16:396–97) For a description of the House of the Cordeliers, its buildings, and its curriculum, see Laure Beaumont-Maillet, *Le Grand Couvent des Cordeliers de Paris: Etude historique et archeologique du XIIIᵉ siècle à nos jours* (Paris: Honoré Champion, 1975). Scholars are learning more about the mendicant program of study and its relationship to the University of Paris.

5. Nicholas undoubtedly lectured regularly at the Franciscan *studium generale* in Paris after he finished his lectureship at the university.

6. The best outlines of the sources for Lyra's career are still the articles cited above by Labrosse, *EF* 16:388–96, and Langlois, "Nicholas de Lyre," pp. 355–67.

7. Nicholas de Lyra, *Oratio ad Honorem S. Francisci,* in *Sancti Francisci Assisiatis: Opera Omnia,* ed. Iohannis de la Haye (Paris: Rouillard, 1641) (not paginated). The *Oratio,* a commentary on Ps 136, was the last of his works.

8. See Jürgen Miethke, *Ockhams Weg zur Sozialphilosophie* (Berlin: de Gruyter, 1969), p. 350.

9. See especially Malcom D. Lambert, *Franciscan Poverty: The Doctrine of the Absolute Poverty of Christ and the Apostles in the Franciscan Order, 1210–1323* (London: S.P.C.K., 1961).

10. Francis himself called the Rule "the book of life, the hope of salvation, the marrow of the Gospel, the way of perfection, the key to Paradise, and the agreement of a perpetual covenant"; Thomas of Celano, "The Second Life of St. Francis," in *St. Francis of Assisi: First and Second Life of St. Francis,* ed. Placid Hermann (Chicago: Franciscan Herald Press, 1963), p. 208.

11. Alexander, Minorita. *Expositio in Apocalypsim,* ed. Alois Wachtel, MGH, Quellen zur Geistesgeschichte des Mittelalters, 1 (Weimar: Hermann Böhlaus,1955; repr. Munich: MGH, 1983); henceforth, Alexander. I will be referring to this important work throughout this translation.

12. Bernard McGinn, *Apocalyptic Spirituality: Treatises and Letters of Lactantius, Adso of Montier-En-Der, Joachim of Fiore, The Franciscan Spirituals, Savonarola,* Classics of Western Spirituality (New York: Paulist Press, 1979), p. 152.

13. John of Parma, his successor, Bonaventure, and Peter John Olivi held that St. Francis was the angel of the sixth seal (Rv 7:2), showing how apocalyptic eschatology influenced Franciscan leaders and theologians.

14. See Marjorie Reeves, "The Development of Apocalyptic Thought: Medieval Attitudes," in *The Apocalypse in English Renaissance Thought and Literature: Patterns, Antecedents, and Repercussions*, eds. C. A. Patrides and Joseph Wittreich (New York: Cornell University Press, 1984), p. 55.

15. Bernard McGinn, *Visions of the End: Apocalyptic Traditions in the Middle Ages* (New York: Columbia University Press, 1979), p. 160.

16. Ibid., p. 151.

17. Lambert, *Franciscan Poverty*, p. 314.

18. McGinn, *Visions of the End*, pp. 203–04.

19. See Warren Lewis, "Peter John Olivi: Prophet of the Year 2000: Ecclesiology and Eschatology in the *Lectura Super Apocalipsim*, Introduction to a Critical Edition of the Text" (Ph.D. diss., Tübingen, 1976). See also David Burr, "The Persecution of Peter John Olivi," *Transactions of the American Philosophical Society*, n.s., 66, Part 5 (1976).

20. Burr, "Persecution," pp. 83–84; see also McGinn, *Visions of the End*, pp. 203–15.

21. After an investigation into the issue of "poor use" prior to the Council of Vienne (1309–12), Clement, in an attempt to avoid a schism in the order, allowed the practice of poverty to be emphasized. In fact, both Clement and the minister general, Alexander of Alexandria, elected in 1313, were moderately conciliatory toward the Spirituals. See Burr, "Persecution," p. 81; see also John Moorman, *A*

History of the Franciscan Order from Its Origins to the Year 1517 (Oxford: Clarendon, 1968), pp. 308–09.

22. Moorman, *History of the Franciscan Order*, p. 311. Central charges in an important papal bull regarded the Olivian distinction between the carnal church, led by the pope and other prelates, and the spiritual Church, to which real authority would be passed. Errors concerning the coming of Antichrist and the end of the age were also condemned; Burr, "Persecution," p. 81.

23. Burr, "Persecutions," pp. 83–87; Lambert, *Franciscan Poverty*, pp. 221–23; and Joseph Koch, "Process gegen die Apokalypsen-Postillle Olivis," *Recherches de Théologie ancienne et médiévale* 5 (1933): 302–15.

24. Burr, "Persecution," p. 83.

25. Moorman, *History of the Franciscan Order*, p. 316.

26. Étienne Baluze, *Miscellanies*, vol. 3, ed. Giovan Mansi (Lucca: J. Riccomini, 1762), pp. 208–09. Langlois,"Nicholas de Lyre," p. 358; Moorman, *History of the Franciscan Order*, p. 316; and Luke Wadding, *Annales Minorum seu trium ordinum a S. Francisco institutorum*, vol. 6 (Quaracchi: Collegium S. Bonaventurae, 1931), p. 396.

27. The first, *Ad conditorum;* the second, *Cum inter nonnullos,* Moorman, *History of the Franciscan Order*, p. 317.

28. Burr, "Persecution," pp. 86–87.

29. Palémon Glorieux, *Répertoire des maitres en théologie de Paris au XIIIe siècle*, vol. 2 (Paris: Vrin, 1933), p. 215.

30. Palémon Glorieux, "Discussiones: D'Alexandre de Hales à Pierre Auriol, La suite des maitres Franciscains de Paris au XIIIe siècle," *Archivum Franciscanum Historicum* 26 (1933): 281.

---

31. After 1331 this question on the Jews was revised by Lyra as a separate tract and was frequently published at the end of later editions of his works. See Hailperin, *Rashi and the Christian Scholars*, pp. 139–40, 285–86; Langlois, "Nicholas de Lyre," pp. 357, 369, 376.

32. Glorieux, "La suite des maitres," p. 262; Labrosse, *EF* 16:388 and 17:595.

33. Labrosse, *EF* 17:596.

34. Burr, "Persecution," p. 85. Sometime in the year 1318 Olivi's grave, which was venerated in Provence, was furtively emptied, probably by the Franciscan hierarchy; his remains were never to be located again (ibid., p. 86).

35. Peter Auriol's commentary on the Apocalypse comprises more than one third of his *Compendium sensus litteralis totius divinae Scripturae*, ed. Phillberto Seeboeck, O.F.M. (Quaracchi: Collegium S. Bonaventurae, 1896); henceforth, Peter. For an excellent discussion of Peter Auriol's importance in the late Middle Ages, see Katherine Tachau, *Vision and Certitude in the Age of Ockham: Optics, Epistemology, and the Foundations of Semantics, 1250–1345* (New York and Leiden: Brill, 1988), p. 85.

36. For example, when in 1319 Blanche, the daughter of Philip the Fair, took the veil, Lyra attended the ceremony as the provincial minister of France; Labrosse, *EF* 16:391–92.

37. Nicholas provided historians with a valuable guide by regularly dating his works. See Langlois, "Nicholas de Lyre," pp. 372–74 for the order of publication. This does not mean that he began his commentaries in 1322. Lyra edited his works frequently and undoubtedly edited lectures on the books. He commented on Daniel, the Psalms, and perhaps the Apocalypse before he began his *magnum opus*. See ibid., p. 370.

38. Although dedications to the pope and such presentations had to do more with custom and ambition than with loyalty, it is important to note here that, in spite of John XXII's interventions in the order and Lyra's love for the French royalty, nowhere does Nicholas either compromise his academic integrity for papal policies or show disloyalty to the papacy. Lyra belonged to the majority of the order who seem to have done everything possible to comply with papal policies while still attempting to maintain their integrity as Franciscans. H. Denifle and E. Chatelain, eds., *Chartularium Universitatis Parisiensis*, vol. 2 (Paris: Delalain, 1897), p. 431, note 4; and Labrosse, *EF* 17:603.

39. Labrosse, *EF* 17:602–03.

40. In 1327 John XXII had summoned Michael to Avignon and detained him there. With William of Ockham, Michael escaped during the night of May 26–27, 1328, from Avignon. They joined Louis the Bavarian at Pisa. Marsilius of Padua was already in the retinue of this opponent of John XXII. During the balance of his life, Michael bitterly attacked the new minister general and the curia with numerous polemical pamphlets. For extensive notes on the sources, see Hans-Georg Beck et al., *From the High Middle Ages to the Eve of the Reformation*, vol. 4 of *History of the Church*, ed. Hubert Jedin, trans. Anselm Biggs (New York: Crossroad, 1986), pp. 373–74.

41. Moorman, *History of the Franciscan Order*, pp. 318–24; Langlois, "Nicholas de Lyre," p. 359.

42. Prologue to the *Postilla Moralitates*, cited in Migne, *PL* 113: 35, 36, and Langlois, "Nicholas de Lyre," p. 380.

43. Labrosse, *EF* 17:602–03; Langlois, "Nicholas de Lyre," p. 359.

44. Langlois, "Nicholas de Lyre," pp. 357–58.

45. Moorman, *History of the Franciscan Order*, p. 317. See also my article, "Many Readers but Few Followers: The Fate of Nicholas of

Lyra's *Apocalypse Commentary* in the Hands of his Late-Medieval Admirers," *Church History*, vol. 64, no. 2 (June, 1995): 185–201.

46. See Bernard McGinn, "Revelation," in *The Literary Guide to the Bible,* ed. Robert Alter and Frank Kermode (Cambridge, Mass.: Harvard Univ. Press, 1987), p. 534.

47. Not all the Franciscans followed Joachim's method rigorously; for many of the early Franciscans, he served as one authority among others, and they blended his method with the earlier Tyconian and Augustinian approach; see David Burr, "Mendicant Readings of the Apocalypse," in *The Apocalypse in the Middle Ages*, ed. Richard Emmerson and Bernard McGinn (Ithaca, N.Y.: Cornell University Press, 1992), p. 94.

48. See David Steinmetz, "Luther and Tamar," *Consensus: A Canadian Lutheran Journal of Theology* 19, No. 1 (1993): 131.

49. See the body of the commentary for bibliographical information about these sources.

The Postilla of Nicholas of Lyra on the Apocalypse of St. John, the Apostle

Chapter 1
THE PREFACE

1. **The revelation of Jesus Christ** . . . This book is divided into two parts, a preface (*proemium*) and a treatise (*tractatum*), which begins in chapter seven.[1] In the preface [John] does three things: first he declares that the hearers be attentive, second that they be faithful, at the place: **John to the seven churches** (1:4), and third teachable or learned, at the place: **I John** (1:9). These three things are usually done in prologues. The first, John does twice: first, due to the authority and the difficulty of the teaching; second, due to its usefulness, at the place: **Blessed is the one who reads** (1:3). People are accustomed to attend to these two things.

Concerning the first, one should know, as was said at the beginning of the Psalms, that the prophetic revelation accompanied by an imaginary vision described in this book (John had imaginary visions and understood what they signified) is of a higher grade when some person appears to instruct about the mysteries, than if it were done without such an apparition—the higher the person appearing, the higher the level of the revelation since an angelic person is higher than a human and a divine is higher than an angelic.[2] Although an angel appears to John instructing him in the Apocalypse, he appeared representing the person of the son of God incarnate and speaking in his person, as will be more clear later. On account of this, the revelation in this book is especially difficult but authentic. This is what is said: **The revelation of Jesus Christ,** The revelation made in the person of Jesus Christ said in this way. **Which God gave him** The Father, because the son possesses divinity from the Father **To make known** That is, to show. **To his servants** To the devoted, to the faithful, and to the studious. **What must soon take place;** Namely, the tribulations of the church which must soon happen, because this proceeds from divine command which is not able to be frustrated. This is for the testing of the faithful and for the increase of their glory. **And by sending his angel** Appearing in this manner. **He made it known** That is, to show. **To his servant** That is, to the evangelist.

2. **Who testified to the word of God** In the beginning of his Gospel with respect to his eternal emanation saying, "In the beginning was the Word and the Word was with God and the Word was God" (Jn 1:1); with respect to his temporal incarnation, saying, "And the Word was made flesh, etc." (Jn 1:14). Therefore, he adds: **And to the testimony of Jesus Christ,** That is, concerning Jesus Christ. **To all that he saw.** In his way of life, in his miracles, in his death and resurrection, as he makes clear in the outline of his Gospel.

3. **Blessed** Here he tells the hearers to be attentive to the usefulness of the book; that is, the attainment of blessedness, saying: **Blessed is the one who reads** Referring to the doctors, **And are those who hear**

Referring to industrious students,[3] **The words of this prophecy,** By keeping in mind. **And who keep what is written in it;** By patiently bearing the future tribulations, and the reason is added: **For the time is near.** Passing quickly, as if to say, the labor of suffering is brief and the reward of blessedness eternal.

4. **John** Here he addresses the willing hearers, and it is divided in two parts, because first, he makes a proposition; second, he answers an unspoken question, at the place: **Look! He is coming** (1:7). The first, he does because he desires spiritual and eternal blessings for them, saying: **John to the seven churches.** This "seven" is understood as the universal Church established in the world. St. Gregory says in Homily 25: "Because in seven days all time is comprehended; the number seven is a proper figure for the whole."[4]

Grace to you In the present life. **And peace** In the future, for there the human desire will be totally stilled. **From him who is** That is, from the eternal God. According to Boethius in the *Consolation of Philosophy*, "Eternity is endless life possessed all at once in its totality and its perfection."[5] Nevertheless, his simplicity is not apprehended by us except by a comparison to time; for we understand in terms of succession and time. For he assists at every time, even infinitely as it were; therefore, this is expressed to us through the distinctions of present, past, and future time. **And from the seven spirits** That is, from all of the angels who are ministers of our salvation. **Who are before his throne,** Prepared to follow his will.

5. **And from Jesus Christ, the faithful witness,** Of the Father's glory and majesty, as is clear in the Gospel. **The firstborn . . . ,** That is, the first among those rising

from the dead, although before him Lazarus and many others were resuscitated from death. This, nevertheless, was to mortal life, which is more properly called death than life, as St. Gregory says in Homily 25, "The true resurrection is to immortal life to which Christ rose first. His resurrection is the cause of the resurrection of others."[6] **And the ruler of the kings on earth.** On account of this he said in his resurrection, "All power is given unto me in heaven and on earth" (in the last chapter of Mt).[7]

. . . Who loved us and freed us That is, who alone by his love and not by our merits washed us. **From our sins** Original and actual. **By his blood,** The sacraments of baptism and penance, by which original and actual sin are abolished, are made efficacious by his blessed passion.

6. **And made us to be a kingdom,** That is, to be written as citizens of the kingdom of heaven. **Priests . . .** Offering sacrifices of praise acceptable to him. **His God** That is, to the whole Trinity. **And Father,** To whom he grants all the glory. **To him be glory** In himself. **And dominion** Over all things. **Forever and ever. Amen.** That is, eternally.

7. **Look! He is coming with the clouds;** Here he responds to a certain implicit question, by which it is possible to ask when the blessed life that John sees for them will be given to the faithful. The response is that in the final judgement the blessed will be whole in body and in spirit, and it is expected quickly but is not to be compared to eternity. Therefore, he says: **Look! He is coming** Concerning the nearness. **With the clouds;** Thus he comes to judgement. "They will see the son of man coming in the clouds of heaven with great power and majesty" (Mt 24:30). **Every eye will see him,** In the

judgement he will appear in human form visible to everyone, and therefore it is added: **Even those who pierced him;** That is, the Jews, who crucified him by word and the soldiers by hand and Pilate by judging.[8] Nevertheless, the vision will be especially delightful to the just, because the savior will come to them. Concerning his coming to the judgement, Luke says in chapter 21:28, "Now when these things begin to take place, stand up and raise your heads"; that is, "Lift up your hearts," as the blessed Gregory says in Homily 1, "Since your redemption draws near."[9] Nevertheless, it will be terrible for the impious, because punishment will come to them; therefore it is added: **And on his account all the tribes of the earth will wail.** That is, all whose hearts are fixed on earthly affections. **Even so, Amen.** *Etiam* is the adverb of affirmation in Latin and similarly *Amen* in Hebrew, and by means of this double affirmation it is implied that the truth is not retractable; the reason is provided, when it is said in 1:8: **"I am the A. . ."** My judgement cannot be frustrated or changed. Moreover, **"A and Ω"** are said because "Alpha" is the first letter of the Greek alphabet and "Omega" the last, and through this it is implied that God is the beginning of all effects and the end to which everything is ordained—(Prv 16:4, "The Lord has made everything for its purpose"). Therefore, it is added: **[The first and the last.** (1:18) is the exposition of the preceding passage twice. **Who is and who was and who is to come . . .** This is explained above.

9. **I, John,** Here, consequently, he briefly informs the willing hearer of the method and material of revelation in this book, which is the custom in prologues of books.[10] It is divided in two parts because, first, he treats the place

and time of this revelation; and second, the material and the method, at the place: **And I heard** (1:10). Concerning the first it is said: **I, John, your brother** Not by relationship of the flesh, but by spiritual regeneration through the sacrament of baptism. **Who share with you the persecution,** On account of Christ, he was immersed in a large vat of boiling oil. **The kingdom** Of heaven, to which one must enter by many tribulations (Acts 14:22). **And the patient endurance in Jesus Christ . . .** That is, on account of Jesus, because he gives patience in persecutions.

Then I turned (1:12). This turning makes understandable what is necessary for the apprehension of a divine revelation by turning the mind from the terrestrial to the celestial. **To see whose voice . . .** That is, the bearer of the voice, because the voice in the strict sense is not visible; nevertheless, it is able to be explained thus: **To see whose voice** That is, that I may perceive, as in Ex 20:18, "When all the people witnessed the sounds." **And on turning I saw seven golden lampstands,** meaning the seven churches, as is explained below (1:13): **And in the midst of the seven lampstands I saw one like the Son of Man . . . ,** That is, the angel representing Christ, who is frequently called the Son of Man in the Gospel, as is clear by consideration.

9. **I was on the island called Patmos** He emerged from the vat of boiling oil unscorched as a strong athlete, and anointed, he was sent into exile to the island of Patmos where he wrote the Apocalypse that the Lord revealed; thus he describes the place. **Because of the word of God** Here he explains the cause of his exile—because he chose neither to deny Christ, nor to cease preaching in his name, he was sent into exile. He notes the time of the revelation, when he says:

10. **I was in the spirit** That is, in the ecstasy of mind. **On the Lord's day,** This day was devoted to the contemplation of God and as a result was suitable for the revelation to occur. **And I heard** Here, consequently, the content and mode of the revelation are considered briefly, and it is divided into four parts: first, the description of the revealer; second, the fear of the listener, at the place: **And when I saw him,** (1:17); third, the consolation of the one who is afraid, at the place: **And he placed** (1:17); and fourth, the writer's information, at the place: **"Now write"** (1:19). Concerning the first it is said: **And I heard behind me a loud voice like a trumpet** (1:10) By which the power and the authority of the angel in the person of Christ is designated.

11. **Saying** To me, **"Write in a book what you see"** For the instruction of the faithful. **"And send it to the seven churches, to Ephesus and to Smyrna. . . ."** First he wrote to these seven churches and then consequently to all the others, as was said before and will become clearer below.

13. **And in the midst of the seven golden lampstands I saw one like the Son of Man,** That is, the angel representing Christ, who is frequently called the Son of Man in the Gospel, as is clear by consideration, and it is shown that he who appeared was an angel and not Christ. Therefore, it is not said here that John saw the Son of Man but one like the Son of Man. Moreover, it is said, **In the middle of the lampstands** It means that Christ is in the middle of the churches—among those consecrated in his name, according to which it is said in the last chapter of Mt, "Behold I am with you always to the end of the age" (28:20). **Clothed with a long robe** That is, in a priestly vestment, which is commonly called

an alb. **And around his breast** The girding of the waist means the restriction of the flesh, which is anticipated in the Old Testament. That which is on the breast around the heart means the restraining of the mind, which is anticipated in the New, whence in Mt 5:27, "You heard that it was said of old, 'You shall not commit adultery.' But I say to you that everyone who looks at a woman with lust has already committed adultery with her in his heart."

The appearance of the angel designates the continence that ought to be among the ministers of Christ for the status of the New Testament. One should know, however, that the old law forbade lusting for another's wife (Ex 20:17), "You shall not covet your neighbor's wife." Nevertheless, because it was not punished; nor is it said that it must be openly punished, therefore, it is said in the Gloss for Phil 2, "The old law prohibited the hand, not the spirit, because it was not expressly and effectively prohibited," just as a new law, and what yet is ordinary, is reputed as nothing in Book 2 of the *Physics*.[11]

14. **His head and his hair were white ... ;** The angel appeared in the form of a priest, because he was clothed with a long robe and also appeared in the form of a judge—from his mouth a sharp, two-edged sword came, as is seen below. The maturity in age and in character designated by the whiteness is appropriate for judges and priests; therefore, he appeared in white—otherwise it is inappropriate to be found in white, and for that reason in Song 5:11, where Christ is described as the young bridegroom, his hair is called black: "His locks are palm fronds and black as the raven." **His eyes were like a flame of fire,** For the acute vision of God reaches to know the innermost parts of things (Heb 4:13, "All are naked and laid bare to his eyes").

15. His feet were like burnished bronze, Glowing, therefore he adds: **Refined as in a furnace,** This designates the tormenting pain of the imminent tribulation for the faithful of Christ. **And his voice was like the sound of many waters.** This signifies the power and the authority of the one speaking, just as earlier through the sound of the trumpet; for the same signification is often repeated through this simile.

16. **In his right hand he held seven stars,** That is, the bishops, who are called stars, as it is explained at the end of the chapter, because they are to illumine the Church equally in life and in doctrine (Dn 12: 3), ". . . And those who lead many to righteousness, like the stars forever and ever." The stars are said to be in the right hand of Christ, because without him they are not able to work justly (Jn 15:5), "Apart from me you can do nothing." Christ says this to the apostles, whose successors are the bishops in the Church of God, as it is said in the *Decretal* (Dist. 21, ca. "In novo Testamento").[12] **And from his mouth came a sharp, two-edged sword,** That is, a just sentence. **And his face was like the sun shining with full force.** "For he is the true light that enlightens everyone coming into the world" (Jn 1:9).

17. **When I saw him, I fell at his feet.** Here, consequently, the fear of John is noted, when it is said: **When I saw him,** This, moreover, was done to show human fragility in the face of angelic power. A parallel case concerns Daniel in the angelic vision of Dn 10. This, nevertheless, holds a greater place in the program, because the angel appeared representing the divine person, as was noted above, who exceeds the angelic incomparably. **And he placed his right hand** Here,

consequently, the consolation of the fearful one is addressed, when it is said: **And he placed his right hand upon me,** In order to comfort my fragility. Therefore, it is added: **"Do not be afraid;"** And he adds the reason: **"I am the first and the last."** By this it is signified what was noted above: **"I am the 'A' and 'Ω'"** (1:8) It is similarly explained, as if he says, "I am strong to save you, therefore do not be afraid." **"And I was dead,"** In his assumption of humanity for the salvation of humankind, on account of which you should not fear. **"And I am alive forever and ever;"** Because Christ, the man, rose to immortal life. **"And I have the keys of Death. . . ."** That is, the power of leading the just from thence, which he also did in his own resurrection, and the power to shut up the impious there, which he will specifically do at the last judgement, saying that terrible word, "Depart you evil ones into the eternal fire" (Mt 25:41).

19. **"Now write"** Here, consequently, the writer's information is placed, in which the material of this book is treated in general, when it is said, **"Now write what you have seen,"** That is, the apparition already described. **"What is,"** That is, the tribulation of the Church already begun, and concerning the end of the world, which is imminent; therefore, it is added: **"And what is to take place. . . ."** In future tribulations to test the elect.

20. **"As for the mystery of the seven stars"** That is, the mystery signified through them, which is explained when it is said: **"The seven stars are the angels of the seven churches,"** That is, their bishops, as the angel who was sent interprets. This is the name of the episcopal office, just as it says in Mal 2:7, "For the lips of the priest should guard knowledge, and the people should seek

instruction from his mouth, for he is the messenger of the Lord of hosts." The bishop is the principal priest in a diocese, whence the highest priest is called the supreme instructor among the ministers of God. **"And the seven golden lampstands"** Just as lampstands uphold lamps, so the doctors of the Church who are the lamps of the church should be upheld by the good deeds of the church. They are called golden because this rule ought to be accomplished by charity, which is signified by gold. Just as gold excels all other metals, so charity exceeds all other gifts of God (1 Cor 13), "For the greatest of these is charity."

Notes

1. For explanations of the technical terms used in medieval biblical commentaries see Alistair J. Minnis, *Medieval Theory of Authorship: Scholastic Literary Attitudes in the Later Middle Ages,* 2nd ed. (Philadelphia: University of Pennsylvania Press, 1988); and A. J. Minnis and A. Brian Scott, *Medieval Literary Theory and Criticism, c. 1100–c. 1375: The Commentary* (Oxford: Clarendon, 1988).

2. In the prologue to the *Commentary on the Psalter* in *The Literal Postill* Nicholas includes a *quaestio,* "On whether David was the most excellent of the prophets." See also St. Augustine's *Literal Meaning on Genesis*, Book 12 (*PL* 34:245–486), trans. John Hammond Taylor in Ancient Christian Writers vols. 41–42 (New York: Newman Press, 1982).

3. One wonders if he is referring to the classroom setting at the Franciscan *Studium generale* in Paris.

4. The numbering system in the *PL* edition is different from the one Nicholas uses for Gregory's sermons, as will be noted. See Sermon 33 on the Gospels on Lk 7:36–50 (*PL* 76:1239C).

5. This is Boethius's famous definition of eternity from Book 5, 6 "Divine Foreknowledge of Human Actions," of *On the Consolation of Philosophy*. See Boethius. *Anicii Manli Severini Boethii Philosophiae consolatio*, ed. Ludwig Bieler, Corpus Christianorum Series Latina, vol. 94 (Turnholt: Brepols, 1957), pp. 90–105.

6. This reference is also not in sermon 25; the Basel 1498 edition of the *Literal Postill* indicates Sermon 35, but it is also not there and was not able to be located.

7. Nicholas frequently refers to a biblical passage in this way.

8. This is an interesting comment that attributes responsibility for the death of Jesus to more than the Jews; Alexander also includes Pilate though not the soldiers; See Alexander, p. 99.

9. Gregory the Great, Sermon 1 of the *Sermons on the Gospels* Lk 21:25–32 (*PL* 76:1437B).

10. See Minnis, *Medieval Theory of Authorship*, p. 315.

11. This source was not found.

12. See Emil Albert Friedberg, *Corpus iuris canonici*, 2nd ed. (Lipsiae: Bernhardi Tauchnitz, 1879–81), Part I, e.g.: c 2, D. XXI, pp. 60–70.

Chapter 2
THE TREATISE BEGINS
INSTRUCTION OF THE SEVEN CHURCHES

1. **"To the angel of the church in Ephesus"** The preface ended, the treatise begins, and it is divided into two parts: first, the seven churches are instructed specifically; second, the whole Church is instructed

generally (chapter 4).[1] The first is divided into seven parts with respect to the seven churches, which will become clear. In the first part the church of Ephesus is instructed, whose commendation is given in advance, so that the subsequent correction would be received better: **"But I have this against you,"** (2:4). In the first part it is said: **"To the angel of the church in Ephesus"** That is, its bishop, just as it was said and may be understood in what is to follow. By instructing the bishop who is the head of that church he also instructs the people who are under him, as will appear in the following. Moreover, the expositors commonly say that it was Timothy, the disciple of Paul, who established the see of Ephesus, just as it was said before concerning 1 Tm 1.[2] Nevertheless, St. Timothy was the apostle over all the bishops of Asia whose churches he founded and ruled, as it is held in *On the Lives of Illustrious Men*; nevertheless, he generally remained in Ephesus. **"These are the words of him who holds the seven stars"** It is explained as above.

2. **"I know your works,"** That is, I approve. **"Your toil"** That is, the tribulation from the adversaries of the faith. **"And your patient endurance."** In the tribulation raised up for you. **"And because you are not able to tolerate evildoers,"** By communing with them, but you reject them from the fellowship of the faithful lest they too be corrupted by their evil. **"You have tested those"** By considering their results from their life and teaching. **"Who claim to be apostles"** That is, sent by Christ to teach the people. **"But are not,"** They are not truly sent by Christ but are subverters of the faithful like Ebion, Cerinthus, and the rest of the heretics who surfaced in Asia and, similarly, the false apostles who said that they

were sent by the apostles, Peter and James, who remained in Jerusalem. Under this pretext, they taught falsely that the observance of the law together with the Gospel was necessary for salvation, as is clear above in the epistles of Paul in many places. **"And have found them to be false."** Not only in doctrine, but also in life, because they simulate an exterior sanctity better to deceive the simple.

3. **". . . And you are enduring patiently"** In the tribulations which they have incited against you. **"And bearing up for the sake of my name,"** Not for vain glory.

4. **"But I have this against you,"** Here the correction is added, and so that the commendation is carried better, it is added at this place: **"But I have this"** Concerning the first it is said: **"But I have this against you,"** The defect must be corrected which is added when it is said: **"The love you had at first"** That is, the works of charity, which you had at the beginning of your conversion. **"You have abandoned."** What was said above appears here, namely, that the word of God is directed to the bishop not only for himself but also for the people under him. Since Timothy was Paul's special and favored disciple, it is likely not that he became deficient in spiritualities but, rather, that he became more proficient. Therefore, this concerns the people under him. They were accustomed to sustain the poor Christians fervently and devotedly; they sent alms to the faithful living in Jerusalem and had sold their possessions to support those believing in Christ, as is clear in Acts 4, and this fervor had grown cold. Therefore, it does not say that the Church had simply abandoned charity, but, the first, that is, the level of fervor held earlier, to which it returns when it is said:

5. **"Remember then from what you have fallen;"** That is, from so great a degree of charity; **"Repent,"** From the omission of so much good. **"And do the works you did at first."** That is, as fervently and as devotedly as at first. It is clear that by the term, "angel," the holy angel is not to be understood here, namely, the guardian of the church of Ephesus (as some have wanted to say);[3] the holy angels are not able to fall from their level of perfection. **"If not,"** That is, if you do not repent, **"I will come to you"** To punish you. **"And remove your lampstand"** By taking away your subjects from your obedience, as some have explained.[4] But this does not seem to be right, because in this way the sin reflects primarily on the bishop and not on the people, which is improbable. Therefore, it is possible to be said that the cooling of the first charity mentioned previously happened at the time not of so great a teacher as St. Timothy but of another succeeding him. At that time the bishops were holy, and those who were in command over their people were the first to be led into torments, and thus the bishops changed frequently. Those who say that Timothy is understood to be the Angel of Ephesus are moved to this because no one more excellent than he was found at the time to rule the church of Ephesus; the opposite conclusion, however, should be drawn, because at the time of an excellent prelate, fewer transgressions happen among the people in the Church. Therefore (I submit myself to better judgement), it seems better to say that it was someone other than St. Timothy.[5]

6. **"But this is to your credit:"** Here the commendation is added as in the custom of the good Samaritan, who poured the gentle oil after the biting wine, when it is

said: **"But this is to your credit:"** Namely, is good and worthy of commendation. **"You hate the work of the Nicolaitans,"** He does not say the Nicolaitans but, rather, their deeds, because persons are esteemed because of love but their faults are hated. This Nicolas was in the primitive church and had an especially beautiful wife, and it was said of him that he was zealous for her. To show the contrary he fell into a worse sin, according to the poet, "He fell into Scylla wishing to avoid Charybdis." He introduced his wife to other Christians saying erroneously that spouses should be shared as other things. It is said in *The Historia Scholastica,* Book 3, Chapter 19, and Clement of Alexandria teaches the same in Book 3 of *The Stromateis* that Nicolas himself lived a holy and chaste life, but others who were incontinent said this.

7. **"Let anyone who has an ear"** Capable of understanding. **"Listen"** That is, let a person desire with the mind. **"To what the Spirit"** Here it is clear, that, although the word is first directed to the church at Ephesus, it is directed to all others established throughout the world, as has been said above. **"To everyone who conquers,"** The world, the flesh, and the devil. **"I will give permission to eat from the tree of life"** That tree is Christ, as is held at the end of the book, whom the blessed enjoy. For the interior is refreshed by his divinity and the exterior by his humanity; therefore, Augustine says concerning this on Jn 10:9 "Whoever enters by me will be saved, and will find pasture."[6]

8. **"And to the angel"** This is the second part of the first part in which the church of Smyrna is instructed whose commendation is placed here, when it is said: **"And to the angel of the church in Smyrna"** This was

commonly held by the doctors to be St. Polycarp. **"These are the words of the first"** It is explained as above.

9. **"I know your affliction"** I approve your patience in it. **"And your poverty,"** In temporalities. **"Even though you are rich."** In spiritualities. **". . . And the slander"** Against the truth. **". . . But are a synagogue of Satan."** Because they are obstinate in their infidelity against Christ, as it is said in the *Church History*, Book 4, Chapter 12: In the city of Smyrna many Jews lived who incited the Gentiles to persecute the Christians. In this persecution many were not only robbed of their things but also crowned with martyrdom—among whom St. Polycarp was thrown into the fire, and, when the fire did not harm him, he was struck with a sword and departed to God.[7]

10. Therefore it is added: **"Do not fear"** That is, protected by me, you will cross to glory through martyrdom. **"Beware, the devil is about to throw . . ."** To do this, he will incite the infidels. **"That you may be tested,"** To be tested as gold in a furnace. This test, moreover, is not the intention of the devil; he does not intend good for those he oppresses, but it is God's intention to draw the good from evil things. By the cruelty of tyrants he lifts up the patience and the crown of the martyrs.

"And for ten days you will have affliction." This is explained in many ways: in one way by referring to the tribulations of the Church generally, signified here by ten days; in another manner the tribulation of ten days signifies a perfect tribulation, because a *denarius* is a perfect number and the first distinction of numbers; the following numbers are replications of ten and of its parts, as it is said in Book 3 of *The Physics*.[8] For eleven is one and ten; twelve is two and ten, and so forth to twenty, which is two-times ten. Thirty is three-times ten, and so forth. In another way, it refers to the ten laws of the Decalogue. That is, the tribulation of the Church will last as long as the observance of the laws of the Decalogue, which is to the end of the world. It is also possible to be explained in another way (saving better judgement), so that the ten days are understood as ten years, according to Ez 4:6 "One day for each year." Perchance the persecution of the church of Smyrna lasted that long. **"Be faithful"** That is, firm in faith. **"Unto death,"** To endure by the faith itself. **"And I will give you the crown of life."** That is, where death does not have a place.

11. **"Let anyone who has an ear . . ."** It is explained as above. **". . . Will not be harmed by the second death."** That is, by hell, called the second death in chapter 21.

12. **"And to the angel"** This is the third part, which includes the instruction to the church of Pergamum; first, their goodness is commended so that the correction of their evil will be better received—considered at the place: **"But I have a few things against you:"** (2:14). Concerning the first it is said: **"And to the angel of the church in Pergamum"** That is, to St. Polycarp, as the doctors commonly say. **"These are the words of the one who has the sword:"** That is, a two-edged sword, just as was noted in chapter 1:16.

13. **"I know where you are living,"** Namely, in the virtue of persecution. Therefore, it is said: **"Where Satan's throne is."** His power in leading the infidels to persecute the Church. **"Yet you are holding fast to my name,"** In faith and practice. **"And you did not deny my faith"** In the persecutions and torments. **"Even"** That is.

"In the days of Antipas" This martyr is specifically named, because by his word and example he inspired others to martyrdom.

14. **"But I have"** Here the correction of their evil is included, when he says: **"But I have a few things against you:"** Namely, sins which must be corrected.

15. **"You have there"** In the church of Pergamum. **"Some who hold to the teaching of Balaam,"** This story is in Nm 25 where it is said that Balak, King of Moab, as a result of Balaam's teaching sent beautiful maidens into the Hebrew camp to tempt the lecherous Hebrews by their beauty. Thus, God was angered against the people. Certain expositors say that in the church of Pergamum there were some who by word and example led others to fornication, as if it were permitted, and to eat food sacrificed to idols. They say also that there were some holding and teaching the error of Nicolas discussed earlier. But this does not seem true, because, if there had been such, it would not be said in the text: **"I have a few things against you"** But many. On account of this, it seems better to say that in the church of Pergamum only some practiced the error of Nicolas, as it is said in the text, and the teaching of Balaam is brought in only as a similitude or as an example. And on account of this, submitting myself to better judgement, this is the how the letter should be explained: **"You have some who hold to the teaching of Balaam"** Not in reality, but in similitude, just as a large man through a certain similitude is called Alexander. And this is the meaning, it seems, of what follows: **"Therefore you have"** As if it says Balak clearly held the evil teaching of Balaam, and thus there are those among you holding the error of Nicolas.

16. **"Repent then."** Just as it was said concerning the church of Ephesus whose first love had been lost. **"If not,"** That is, if in any way you neglect to amend these things, **"I will come to you soon"** In the final judgement, which is especially near compared to eternity. On account of which it is said in 1 Jn 2:18, "It is the last hour." **"And will make war against them"** Against their stubborn error. **"With the sword of my mouth."** That is, with that horrible sentence, "You that are accursed depart into the eternal fire" (Mt 25:41).

17. **"Let anyone who has an ear listen. . . ."** It is explained as above. **"To everyone who conquers I will give manna,"** Manna figuratively; clearly it was given corporeally to the children of Israel in the desert (Ex16), but the true manna is he himself, who says in Jn 6, "Very truly, I tell you, it was not Moses who gave you the bread from heaven, but it is my Father who gives you the true bread from heaven." And it is added, "I am the bread of Life." This is the heavenly manna that refreshes the saints inside and outside, as was said previously, and it is called "hidden" to persons of this present life, according to which it is said in Ps 31:19, "Oh how abundant is your goodness that you have laid up for those who fear you."

"And I will give to everyone a white stone," That is, a body decorated with a property of clarity, and it is called a stone or a pebble because it is extracted from the earth just as a jewel. **"On the stone a new name"** Anyone who is blessed clearly and bodily by the properties of this glorious body will be written into the celestial city. **"That no one knows except the one who receives it."** According to which it is said in 1 Cor 2:9, "'No eye has seen, nor ear heard, nor the human heart conceived, what

God has prepared for those who love him'." For the enormity of this sweetness is not knowable by pilgrims but understood by those who have already received it.

18. **"And to the angel:"** This is the first part of the section in which the church of Thyatira is instructed. And it is divided into three parts because first its commendation is placed; second the reprimand of evils, at the place: **"But I have"** (2:20); third the distinction of the good from evil, at the place: **"But to the rest of you"** (2:24).

Concerning the first part, it is said: **"And to the angel of the church in Thyatira:"** Some call this angel St. Irenaeus, who illumined not only the church in Thyatira but also many others in his life and teaching, and he went all the way to Lyons, a city in Gaul.[9] This, however, does not seem probable; first, because he was not a contemporary of St. John, who seems to write to bishops contemporary to him.[10] Irenaeus flourished under Commodus Aurelius, who began to rule in the year 182, as Jerome says in *On the Lives of Illustrious Men*.[11] Second, it is not likely that a bishop of so great a reputation and teaching in his Church would permit the things that are written here. Therefore (I submit myself to better judgement), it seems to me that it was another bishop of lesser reputation and a contemporary of John who ruled the church of Thyatira. **"These are the words of the Son of God,"** The natural son, who is Christ; the rest are adopted. **"Who has eyes"** This is explained as in the first chapter.

19. **"I know"** Through testing. **"Your works—"** In the effect. **"Your faith,"** In the understanding. **"Love,"** In the will. **"Service"** By devotedly serving your God. **"And your patient endurance."** In tribulation. **"And**

your last works are greater than the first." By proceeding from the good to the better.

20. **"But I have"** Here he presents their defects which are noted when it is added: **"You tolerate that woman Jezebel,"** It is certain that it is not that one who in 1 Kgs is called an idolater and a fornicator, because she was trampled by the feet of horses more than four hundred years earlier (2 Kgs 9). Some say that she was the wife of the bishop, but it does not seem likely that a man so good, as was described before, would have such a wife. Therefore, it should be said that she was another false prophet or, by chance, some heretic who is designated figuratively by a female name due to the wantonness of the flesh; frequently a weak and effeminate man is called a woman. **"Who calls herself a prophet"** Nevertheless, falsely. **"And is teaching"** Error. **"And beguiling my servants"** That is, the simple Christians. **"To practice fornication"** Saying that it is permitted. Many have said in error that simple fornication is permitted. Or this is understood concerning the error of Nicolas, who flourished then, as has been said above. **"And to eat food sacrificed to idols."** During the veneration of idols; otherwise it would not be illicit, unless it scandalizes the innocent, as the Apostle teaches in 1 Cor 8.

21. **"I gave her time to repent . . . ,"** She was obstinate; therefore, the punishment is added when it is said:

22. **"And I am throwing her on a bed,"** Of infernal punishment—concerning which it is said in Is 14:11, "Your pomp is brought down to Sheol, your body has fallen; maggots are the bed beneath you, and worms are your covering." **"And those who commit adultery with her"** By communing with her evil. **"Are in great**

distress," That is, in Hell with her. **"Unless they repent
. . . ;"** In the present life.

23. **"And I will strike her children"** That is, her
imitators. **"Dead."** That is, in Hell. **"And all the
churches will know"** Clearly what is hidden. **"That I am
the one who searches minds and hearts,"** That is, exam-
ining and punishing concupiscence and evil thoughts.
"And I will give to each of you as your works deserve."
Punishment to the impious and glory to the just.

24. **"But to the rest of you . . . I say,"** Here the
distinction of the good from evil has been inserted; first,
by instructing them; second, by promising a reward, at the
place: **"To everyone who conquers"** (2:26). Concerning
the first, it is said: **"But to the rest of you in Thyatira,"**
And, who these are, is indicated. **"Who do not hold this
teaching,"** That is, who do not receive the teaching of
Jezebel. **"And who have not learned 'the deep things of
Satan',"** That is, those who do not approve of the
arrogance of Ebion and Cerinthus, who, puffed up with
pride, spoke against the reverence of the person of Christ,
denying his divinity. Therefore, St. John in the beginning
of his own Gospel proclaimed the divinity, as it is said in
On the Lives of Illustrious Men.[12] **"What some call"** Here
the avoidance of another error is dealt with, namely, of
the pseudo-apostles who were saying that the observance
of the laws with the Gospel was necessary, which is called
in Acts 15:10 "An unbearable burden." In relation to this,
John says or, better, the angel appearing to him in the
person of Christ: **"What some call"** Namely, pseudo-
apostles. **"I do not lay on you any other burden;"** That
is, the observation of the law—a burden the false apostles
say that you must bear.

25. **"Only hold fast to what you have"** That is, the true Gospel proclaimed to you by the true apostles. **"Hold"** Firmly. **"Until I come."** To the judgement.

26. **"To everyone who conquers"** Here he instructs those noted before by promising God's reward. **"To everyone who conquers"** The temptations of the world, of the flesh, and of the devil. **"And continues . . . to the end"** That is, to death. **"My works"** This is said, because Jesus first did works and afterwards taught (Acts 1:1). **"I will give authority"** In the final judgement the perfect will judge with Christ, and thus they will have the power to judge the nations.

27. **"To rule them with an iron rod,"** That is, with inflexible justice. **"As when clay pots are shattered—"** Because then sinners will be thrust back into Hell.

28. **"Even as I also received authority"** Everything that the Son has, he has from the Father. **"To that one I will also give the morning star."** That is, a glorious body gleaming with a quality of clarity.

29. **"Let anyone who has an ear listen to what the Spirit is saying to the churches."** This is explained as above.

Notes

1. As Peter Auriol interprets this reference in the Compendium, chapters 2–3 refer specifically to the churches in Asia, and, beginning at chapter 4, the future and hidden secrets of the whole catholic Church are revealed (p. 442).

2. Nicholas comments on this in the *Literal Postill*, on 1 Tm 1:3.

3. This reference does not refer to Alexander or Peter; he has other commentaries at his disposal.

4. See Alexander, p. 25.

5. This idiomatic expression, *salvo meliori judicio,* is a favorite expression of Nicholas when he wants to introduce a critique of the sources he is using. He sometimes uses it with a false humility, sometimes sarcastically, but always in a clever and wise way to introduce his own views.

6. *In Iohannis Evangelium, Tractatus* 45,15. (*PL* 35:1726).

7. Eusebius, *Church History,* 4.15.

8. This numerical symbolism is common to the Middle Ages.

9. Peter (p. 446) and Alexander (p. 34).

10. Alexander, referring to Irenaeus (p. 34), notes that sometimes, as he had promised (4:1), John discusses not contemporaries but figures from the future.

11. Jerome, *De Viris illustribus,* chapter 35 (*PL* 23:875).

12. *De Viris illustribus,* chapter 9 (*PL* 23:843).

Chapter 3
THE INSTRUCTION OF THE SEVEN CHURCHES

1. **"And to the angel of the church in Sardis . . ."**
Some expositors say that this was St. Melito, whom they assert was Bishop of Sardis at that time and was perfected by martyrdom there.[1] They contend this using *Church History*, Book 5, Chapter 24, but, with all due respect,

this is not said there but that he was a eunuch preserving his chastity for the kingdom of heaven and that, filled with the Holy Spirit, he stayed in the city of Sardis waiting for the coming of the Lord. Granting the things that are said concerning him there—that he was a martyr and bishop—this does not confirm their interpretation; on the contrary in the text it is added: **"You have a name of being alive, but you are dead."** Which referring to so saintly a bishop does not seem to be verifiable, nor can it refer to the people under him, because the sins of the subjects reflect on the prelate. At the time of a holy prelate the subject people are more likely to avoid sins. Therefore, it seems better to say that it was another bishop of Sardis who was not so saintly. At that time, as has been said before, bishops changed frequently. The text continues by first offering the reprimand for sins; second the commendation of the few, at the place: **"Yet you have still a few persons"** (3:4).

Concerning the first it is said, **"These are the words of Him who has the seven spirits"** That is, all of the angels assisting Him. **"And the seven stars:"** That is, all of the bishops, as it has been said above in chapter 1. **"I know your works;"** Because nothing is hidden from me. **"You have a name"** Appearing holy and with good reputation. **"But you are dead."** Spiritually, according to the truth.

2. **"Wake up,"** To understand the defect in you and in your flock. **"And strengthen what remains"** That is, those under you by word and example. **"And is on the point of death,"** The people fall into sin easily, unless they are sustained by the word and the example of the prelate. **"For I have not found your works perfect"** That is, rather, defective.

3. **"Remember then what you have received and heard;"** Namely, the teaching of Christ through his true apostles. **"Obey it,"** By deeds. **"And repent."** From the omission of good and the commission of evil. **"If you do not wake up,"** That is, be diligent concerning the things said. **"I will come to you"** In death. **"Like a thief"** Because nothing is more uncertain than the hour of death.

4. **"Yet you still have a few persons. . . ."** Here he commends the few, as if to say, "The multitude of your subjects is not spoiled by sin." **"They will walk with me . . . ,"** Namely, those who are not stained by sin, and the whiteness of the clothing means the robe of glory and of immortality. Because God is no respecter of persons, therefore, it is added:

5. **"If you conquer,"** As if to say, not only these, but everyone who has conquered the world, the flesh, and the devil will be clothed with a robe of glory. **"And I will not blot out your name . . . ;"** The book of life is God's predestination from which, when it is written in it, one's name is not deleted because that one will ultimately be saved; nevertheless, the word "deleted" is used to refer to a person's falling from justice and being rewritten by restorative grace. **"I will confess your name"** That is, the one who is truly Christian.

7. **"And to the angel of the church in Philadelphia:"** Expositors commonly say that this was Quadratus, about whom it is written in *Church History,* Book 4, Chapter 3, that he was a man who was especially skilled in sacred writing and wrote many things to defend the faith of Christ and to confute the infidels.[2] Therefore, it follows that first his commendation is proposed; second the conversion of the infidels through him, at the place:

"**Behold I will make**" (3:9); third the promise, at the place: "**If you conquer,**" (3:12).

Concerning the first, it is said: "**These are the words of the holy one, the true one,**" (3:7) That is, Christ, who is the holy of the holy ones (Dn 9:24) and the truth itself (Jn 14:6), "I am the way, and the truth, and the life." "**Who has the key of David,**" That is, the power to open the understanding of the Scriptures (Lk 24:33, "And he opened to them the sense of the Scriptures"). "**Who opens and no one will shut,**" No one is able to impede those from understanding the Scriptures whom he wishes to instruct; nor can anyone understand the Scriptures except by referring to him.[3]

8. "**I know your works.**" That is, I approve. "**I have set before you an open door,**" That is, to understand the Scriptures. "**Which no one is able to shut.**" That is, to impede you from the truth of doctrine. "**You have but little power,**" As if to say, because I did not give you the grace of miracles, as I did to many other bishops of that time, I have compensated by giving you an excellent understanding of the Scriptures. "**And you have kept my word**" In deed and in teaching. "**And have not denied my name.**" In the persecution of the faithful.

9. "**I will make**" Here the conversion of the infidels through him is introduced; many Jews lived in his diocese, who were converted through his teaching, and this is what is said: "**I will make those of the synagogue of Satan**" That is, some of the Jews whose congregation is called the synagogue of Satan at that time, because after the resurrection of Christ, the ascension, and the preaching of the apostles, they remained in unbelief. "**Who say that they are Jews and are not,**" The

Hebrews were called Jews by ancestry from whom Christ descended according to the flesh, and, therefore, after they denied Christ the reality of this name did not remain but transferred to the Christians from the tribe of Judah, who confessed Christ. They were circumcised by the Spirit and not by the flesh according to Rom 2:28–29, "For a person is not a Jew who is one outwardly, nor is true circumcision something external and physical. Rather, a person is a Jew who is one inwardly, and real circumcision is a matter of the heart—it is spiritual and not literal."

"**I will make them come and bow down**" Because many of the Jews, as has been said, converted to Christ, humbling themselves before his face and his servant Quadratus. "**And they will learn**" Through the illumination of faith. "**That I have loved you.**" By advancing you not only to the catholic faith, but also to the episcopal office.

10. "**Because you have kept my word of patient endurance,**" By word and deed. "**I will keep you from the hour of trial**" From the Roman Emperors ruling in the whole world and wherever they are persecuting the Catholic faith. Nevertheless, contrary to this, it seems that this persecution had already occurred under two emperors, namely, Nero and Domitian, as it is said in the "Legend of St. John, the Evangelist": By the order of Domitian he was sent into exile onto the island called Patmos, where this book was written, and in that same year Domitian was killed. It must be said, therefore, that although the persecution of the Christians by these emperors had passed, the greater persecutions by later emperors were in the future. John speaks of this before it occurred via a future mode. Therefore it is added:

11. **"Behold I am coming soon;"** To receive you. **"Hold fast to what you have,"** That is, the grace given to you. **"So that no one may seize"** For when some fall from justice in the present, others are substituted for them, just as it is clear in the "Legend of the Forty Martyrs," when one of them fell, the jailer was substituted, and received his crown.[4]

12. **"If you conquer,"** Here the promise of reward is offered. This reward, nevertheless, seems to be an increase of grace in the present time. Therefore it says: **"If you conquer,"** Evil. **"I will make you a pillar"** That is, strong and powerful in faith, not only for them, but also for others by comforting and sustaining. According to this mode, Peter and John and James are called pillars (Gal 2:9). **"In the temple of my God;"** That is, in the Church militant as will be clear in the following, **"You will never go out of it."** Neither through apostasy nor through excommunication.

"I will write on you the name of my God," Because in the Scriptures such are called gods (Ps 82:6, "I say, 'You are gods'"), which the Savior explains, when he says in Jn 10:35, "Those to whom the word of God came were called 'gods'." He represents in the Church the person of God. **"And the name of the city"** That is, of the Church militant, which is clear from what follows: **"Which descends . . . from heaven,"** For the Church militant is ruled and ordered by the Holy Spirit. It must be noted that Christ, inasmuch as he was human, speaks naming his God. **"And my own new name."** Because it is called "Christian" from Christ, which name he did not have from the beginning, granted he may have been called "Jesus" at the circumcision (Lk 2), but after the baptism he was called Christ. Similarly, his faithful from the beginning were not called Christians, but only disciples. Thereafter, when the faith spread to Antioch and the faithful multiplied there, they were first called Christians, as it says in Acts 11:26.

14. **"And to the angel of the church in Laodicea:"** This is the seventh part of the first section in which he writes to the Bishop of Laodicea, whom some expositors say was St. Sagaris. They allege this from Book 5 of *Church History*, Chapter 24, but, with all due reverence, a bishop is not mentioned there, but a priest and martyr, and it says that he rests there in peace; moreover, many other bishops are cited in that same place.[5] Even if one wanted to assume this was the bishop of Laodicea, it cannot be held on account of this problem, and, furthermore, the opposite seems the case; for this is what follows in the text:

"Because you are lukewarm, and neither cold nor hot, I am about to spit you out of my mouth." (3:16) It does not seem convenient to apply this to [Sagaris], because in the fervor of love he obtained the crown of martyrdom, nor to the people subject to him for similar reasons mentioned earlier. Therefore (I submit myself to better judgement), I say that this was another bishop of lesser perfection. As has been said earlier, holy bishops were frequently killed or sent into exile, and others who were less devoted succeeded them. Thus it proceeds, and, first the reprimand for sin is noted; second the salutary admonition, at the place: **"I counsel you"** (3:18); third the promise of reward, at the place: **"To the one who conquers"** (3:21).

Concerning the first, **"The words of the Amen,"** (3:14) The adverb is in Hebrew, and signifies the same as "truly," and therefore it is attributed to Christ, who says concerning himself in Jn 14:6, "I am the way and the truth and the life." **"The faithful and true witness,"** Of the paternal majesty, according to which it is said in Jn 3, "We speak of what we know and testify to what we have seen." **"The origin of God's creation:"** For, "All things came into being through him, and without him not one thing came into being" (Jn 1:3).

15. **"I know your works;"** To be imperfect. Therefore it is added: **"Because you are neither cold"** Avoiding transgressions for fear of punishment. **"Nor hot,"** That is, fulfilling my laws with loving fervor.

16. **"But because you are lukewarm,"** That is, slow to the good, disagreeable, and idle. **"I am about to spit you out of my mouth."** That is, to repel you from me, as something abominable; for idleness is at the bottom of the vices.

17. **"Because you say, 'I am rich,'"** In knowledge and in virtue. **"'I have prospered,'"** By teaching doctrine. **"'And I need nothing.'"** To be taught by anyone. **"You do not realize that you are wretched,"** Through the lack of grace. **"Pitiable,"** Through liability to punishment. **"Poor,"** With respect to spiritual goods. **"Blind"** Because you do not see your defects. **"And naked."** That is, deprived of virtues.

18. **"I counsel you"** Here the salutary admonition is introduced, when it is said: **"I counsel you to buy"** With respect to good works. **"Gold refined by fire"** That is, wisdom enkindled by love, otherwise it would be puffed up by pride. But against this the Apostle seems to say in Rom 11:6, "But if it is by grace, it is no longer on the basis of works, otherwise grace would no longer be

grace." Moreover, love is the very same as grace, or is inseparably annexed to it and is not purchased through works. It must be said that grace is received in one mode according to habit by God making the soul acceptable; in another mode according to divine motion by which it moves the soul to the supernatural good, just as by general motion it moves all things to the good things connatural to itself.

Similarly, merit is received in a twofold manner. In one mode by a *condign* merit and in another by a *congruous* merit. Moreover, if grace is received in the first manner and wholly first, it does not fall under *condign* merit, so that the previously cited passage of the Apostle is understood. Nevertheless, having the first grace, on account of works it is merited (*de condigno*) with respect to its increase. In the same way, the first grace falls under *congruous* merit, because, if a person does what is in one by disposing oneself to grace but not without oneself (concerning which it is written in Prv 8: "The will is prepared by the Lord"),[6] it is congruous that God establish it for the person.

If moreover it is received in the second mode, it does not fall under merit but precedes every condign and congruous merit. The divine flows to humans in such a way, as long as they are in the present life; some succeed in this infusion by the exertion of the free will disposing them to the supernatural good. Thus they merit the congruous habitual grace established for them by God and through it its increase (*de condigno*). Others indeed do not succeed, on account of which they deserve to be left by themselves and to fall into sin through the weakness of the free will.[7]

It follows: **"So that you may be rich;"** In divine spiritualities. **"And white robes to clothe you"** That is, in virtues. **"To keep the shame of your nakedness from being seen;"** Before God and the holy angels. **"And salve to anoint your eyes so that you may see."** That is, the grace of the Holy Spirit, who illumines the eyes of the mind. They say **"Anoint"** Because, although grace is given by God alone, it is nevertheless in the power of the person to be given to oneself, because one is able to dispose oneself to it, in a manner of speaking.[8]

19. **"I reprove and discipline those whom I love."** As a father his dear children. **"Be earnest,"** That is, to imitate the good. **"And repent."** From sinning.

20. **"Listen! I am standing at the door,"** Of the human heart. **"Knocking;"** By admonishing towards the supernatural good. **"If you hear my voice"** By confessing my warning. **"And open the door,"** Through the exercise of the free will to the good. **"I will come in to you"** Through justifying grace dwelling in one. **"I will come in to you and eat with you,"** For God is loved in such a person and the self in God.

21. **"To the one who conquers"** Here, at last, the promised reward is placed, when it is said: **"To the one who conquers"** Reviling the world, the flesh, and the devil. **"I will give a place with me on my throne,"** That is, rest in the heavenly kingdom. **"Just as I myself conquered"** Through my suffering. **"And sat down with my Father on his throne"** (Mk 16:19, "He was taken up into heaven and sat down at the right hand of God").

Notes

1. Peter (p. 448) and Alexander (p. 39).

2. Eusebius, *Church History*, Book 5.17.

3. This christological focus is a trademark for Nicholas; neither Alexander nor Peter interprets this passage christologically.

4. See Alexander, p. 44, n. 1.

5. The reference in *Church History* is to a bishop, not a priest. Nicholas seems to be misreading the text.

6. This verse is from Prv 8 in the Septuagint; it is not in the Vulgate. It was frequently cited in the tradition in a discussion of nature and grace.

7. For a good discussion of these distinctions in grace in medieval theology see Heiko Oberman, *Forerunners of the Reformation: The Shape of Late Medieval Thought* (1969; Philadelphia: Fortress, 1981), pp. 123–41.

8. Nicholas usually relies upon Thomas Aquinas for his theological formulations, but here he seems to have moved beyond what Thomas would say about a person's having the power to obtain grace; see Oberman, *Forefunners of the Reformation*, p. 130.

Chapter 4
THE BOOK'S METHOD OF REVEALING
THE WHOLE PROGRESS OF HISTORY

1. **After this I looked,** Having described the vision of St. John, which specifically instructs the seven churches of Asia, although, as a result, all of the other churches are

instructed, these visions instruct the whole Church generally. In the spirit under certain images, he saw the course of history from the time of the apostles to the end of the world, namely, the tribulations, consolations, and notable changes, of which some have already occurred and others are in the future.[1] St. John wrote these imaginary visions; however, he did not express their understanding, even though he understood them fully. Sometimes he inserted the method through which to understand the rest. For example, in chapter 1 he says that the seven golden candles are the seven churches and the seven stars are the seven angels, that is, their bishops; similarly, he says the same in the following, as will be clear in these places, God willing. Rarely, though, is it permitted to understand the mysteries.

The literal understanding is not what is signified by the words immediately, but it is what the images signify, as it is said in Jgs 9:14, "The trees said to the bramble, 'You come and reign over us'." The literal sense does not refer to the trees, or to the timber, but to the men of Shechem, signified by the timber, who made Abimelech king over them.[2] One should also know that these visions are not separated by the time in which they were experienced, because John saw the whole in one day. This is clear in what he says in chapter 1: **I was in the spirit on the Lord's day,** They are distinguished by the times in which they were partly fulfilled and partly unfulfilled, as will be seen better below.

The balance of this book is divided into two parts, because first the mode of the vision is introduced; and second the course of the fulfillment beginning at chapter 6. Concerning the first, one should know that the whole

Trinity reveals the Apocalypse with respect to the human Christ. Christ is the one speaking to John in the character of the angel. As a human, Christ is superior to the angels because of the union with the divine substance and the fullness of grace, although he may be less than the angels by reason of his human nature, as it is said in Heb 2:7.

Therefore, first the majesty of God, who is revealing, is introduced; second the dignity of the human receiving the revelation of Christ in the following chapter. The first is declared from the three, namely, from the imperial throne and from the noble company, at the place: **And around the throne** (4:3) and out of reverent obedience, at the place: **And without ceasing** (4:8). Concerning the first, St. John says: **After this I saw,** Thus he saw imaginatively, as if the door of heaven were opened, by which he means that the course of history was revealed to him, which is called "heaven" in the Scriptures. Gregory says in Homily 37, "The Church of the present time is called the kingdom of heaven, in which the doctor who is accustomed to command is called least. . . ."[3]

And the first voice, In this he indicates the authority of the angel speaking, as it has been said in chapter 1. **"Come up here,"** To see the course of the Church; therefore it is added: **"And I will show you what must take place quickly."** According to God's ordaining, which cannot be frustrated.

2. **At once I was in the spirit,** By understanding the imaginary vision. **And there in heaven stood a throne,** Through this, the authority and power of God ruling the Church is understood. **With one seated on the throne!** Namely, God three and one.

3. **And the one seated there looks like jasper and carnelian,** Such visions occur appropriate to what is

revealed. God appears, as governing the Church militant, because God is its consoler and fire of charity. In the primitive Church God sent the Holy Spirit upon the apostles in the image of fire. Therefore, here it is called the color of jasper; for green is a comforting sight. **And carnelian,** That is, the color red. Because of its similarity to fire, it signifies the fire of charity. **.... And around the throne is a rainbow** The rainbow signifies the covenant between God and the Church. The rainbow is a sign of the covenant between God and the earth (Gn 9). **That looks like an emerald.** An emerald is green in color, and this is one of the colors of the rainbow. Thus this imaginary rainbow appeared with the color green appearing more intense than the rest. This signifies God's future consolation to the elect, especially in the future tribulations of the Church, because the color green is a comforting sight.[4]

4. **Around the throne** Here he describes the majesty of God in the midst of the noble company, when it is said: **Around the throne are twenty-four thrones,** These thrones signify the universal sees of the Church, which, though many, are signified by this number to show a concordance between the Old and New Testaments. In 1 Chr 25, David wishing to increase the worship of God established twenty-four priests in the temple with seven ministries. In the Holy Scriptures a determinate number is frequently placed for an indeterminate one, as was said above in the first chapter where the seven spirits of God are understood as the multitude of the holy angels. Gregory says in Homily 25 that seven demons are metaphors for the universal vices.[5]

And seated on the thrones are twenty-four elders, These designate the universal bishops, who should be mature in age and character. **Dressed in white robes,** In them chastity ought to shine. **With golden crowns on their heads.** In the sensible faculties of their minds, which are called "heads," the clarity of wisdom ought to shine, which the Holy Scriptures frequently call "golden." 5. **Coming from the throne** Of God. **Are flashes of lightning, and rumblings and peals of thunder,** That is, the flash of miracles, the declaration of rewards for good works, and terror for the evil. These three were in the primitive Church, and God later granted them to the prelates of the Church. **And in front of the throne burn seven flaming torches,** The throne of God. **Which are the seven spirits of God;** To explain what is understood in the torches, some take it one way and others another. Some call the seven spirits the seven gifts of the Holy Spirit prepared to be given by their dispensers; therefore, they are said to be before the throne of God.[6] By others the seven spirits are understood as the universality of the holy angels prepared to deliver God's good pleasure, who are called burning torches because they illuminate and enkindle the faithful to understanding and the love of heaven, according to Heb 1:14, "Are not all angels spirits in the divine service?"[7]

6. **And in front of the throne there is something like a sea of glass** That is, the sacrament of baptism. **Like crystal.** Because it is not mobile or fluid, baptism imprints an indelible character and is not repeatable. **Around the throne . . . are four living creatures,** That is, the four evangelists, as some say,[8] but the following line seems to differ, when it is said:

7. **The first living creature is like a lion . . . and the third living creature with a face like a human face,**

Matthew is the latter, as has been said earlier at the beginning of the Gospels, and the holy doctors agree. Matthew, however, is not third in the order of the evangelists but first, and he wrote the first Gospel, as Jerome says in his prologue on Matthew. Therefore, others argue more probably that the four living creatures are the four patriarchates, of which the first is Jerusalem.

In Jerusalem the Church began and resembled a lion because of the constancy of those living there, like Peter and John, who constantly said to the leaders of the Jews, "We must obey God rather than any human authority" (Acts 5:29).

The second patriarchate is Antioch, which is compared to an ox, because it was prepared to obey the commands of the apostles living in Jerusalem as Acts 15 makes clear, and it is there that the disciples were first called "Christians" (Acts 11).

The third is Alexandria, which is compared to a human face. In Alexandria from the beginning there were learned doctors, not only in divine but also in humane letters, such as Pierius,[9] Athanasius, and many others.

The fourth is Constantinople, which is compared to a flying eagle, because there persons were elevated through contemplation, such as Gregory of Nazianzus and many others.

8. **And the four living creatures, each of them with six wings,** The first wing is the natural law; the second the law of Moses; the third the oracles of the prophets; the fourth the message of the councils; the fifth the teaching of the apostles; and the sixth the decrees of the general councils. By these six wings ecclesiasts ought to ascend upwards through the contemplation of divine things and

to descend downwards to the edification of their neighbors; to fly to the right by the benefit of grace in prosperity and to the left by patience in adversity. **Are full of eyes all around and inside.** By considering the present, the past, and the future.

Without ceasing This shows the majesty of God in reverent worship, and first in the patriarchates—the four animals signify the patriarchates. **Day and Night they sing, "Holy,"** In these churches the divine office was first celebrated devotedly both day and night. The three "Holies" designate the persons of the Trinity, and at the same time it is added: **"The Lord God Almighty,"** To signify the unity of essence; three persons are one God, and God omnipotent. **"Who was and is and is to come."** This expresses the eternity of God, which we do not apprehend along the way unless by comparison to distinctions in time, as was said in chapter 1.

9. **And whenever the living creatures . . .** This describes the worship of divine praise in the other cathedral churches established throughout the world, which in celebrating the divine offices ought to follow the order of the four patriarchates, although the Roman Church, which is first, is head of all, and this is what is said: **And whenever the living creatures give glory . . .** By serving and praising God in many kinds of ceremonies and by administering the sacraments.

10. **The twenty-four elders** That is, other cathedral churches conforming to them. **They cast their crowns before the throne,** As a sign of reverence they confess that they have the clarity of virtue and of wisdom, which is designated by the golden crowns, as was said above. **Singing,**

11. **"You are worthy, our Lord and God, to receive glory"** This does not mean that God receives something new or that something new accrues to God, as a result of human works and praises, but that humans who have received benefits from God rise to praise and glorify the excellence of the eternal majesty. **"For you created all things,"** By creating them out of nothing. **"And by your will they existed"** By your disposition from eternity before they were created—just as the material of a house before it is in effect preexists in the mind of the artisan; accordingly this is said in Book 7 of the Metaphysics that a house in matter is from a house which is in the mind.[10] Indeed all things find themselves created before God as things made before the artificer. **"And were created."** That is, produced in time and out of divine will, not out of necessity.

Notes

1. This passage is the *locus classicus* for the historical/sequential method of interpreting the Apocalypse. Alexander Minorita and Peter Auriol both wrote the same comment at this point. The whole course of history is foretold in the Apocalypse in a continuous fashion, and one can read the images of the Apocalypse as a detailed map of the past and the future. Nicholas, of course, will criticize the map reading of his models.

2. Nicholas follows the tradition emphasized by Thomas in *The Summa Theologiae* I[a], Q. 1, a.10 that the literal includes the figurative or parabolic sense.

3. This citation is in Sermon 12 (*PL* 76:1476).

4. One of the major themes of the Apocalypse according to Nicholas and the wider commentary tradition is the future consolation for Christians.

5. Sermon 33 (*PL* 76:1593).

6. Alexander, p. 56.

7. This is close to Peter, but Nicholas is referring to another unidentified tradition here as well.

8. Alexander, for example (p. 59); Peter suggests either the four evangelists or the four patriarchal sees (p. 460). Nicholas will choose the patriarchal sees because he argues the context calls for one over the other.

9. A third-century presbyter at Alexandria who headed the catechetical school in 265 and later lived in Rome.

10. Aristotle, probably from Bk. VII: Ch. 7, but his references to Aristotle are difficult to locate.

Chapter 5
CHRIST (HUMAN AND DIVINE) REVEALS THE COURSE OF HISTORY TO JOHN

1. **Then I saw in the right hand** Here he describes the worthiness of the human Christ, who receives the revelation. First the profundity of the divine secret is advanced; second the difficulty of opening it, at the place: **And I saw** (5:2); third, the dignity of Christ is inferred, at the place, **Then one** (5:5).

Concerning the first it is said: **Then I saw in the right hand** That one sitting is God three and one, as has been said. **A scroll** This book is the divine knowledge, in which all things are written. One should know that in God knowledge is twofold or better unified but described in two modes: (1) the knowledge of the simple idea, which extends itself to all possible things, which never have been nor will be; and (2) the knowledge of vision, which considers the existence of each thing and the distinctions of time, namely the past or the present or the future. These are operative in the power of God, insofar as it operates in time. Such are the things that were revealed to the human Christ and handed down by him to John the Apostle. The operative power of God is called metaphorically his right hand. Because we work with the right hand, therefore the scroll that is called the knowledge of God concerning the things God disposes to do is conveniently said to be in God's right hand.

Sealed This seal designates the closing of the divine knowledge of what God is disposed to do and the revelations which are to be fulfilled by God. **With seven seals;** That is, by every manner of obscurity, as some interpret, and here a determinate number is placed for an indeterminate—evidently seven for the multitude of obscurities. Gregory says in Homily 25: "Mary had seven demons and was filled with all the vices."[1] Nevertheless, this does not fit well with that which follows in the subsequent chapter concerning the opening of the seals, as it proceeds from the first seal to the seventh in a fixed pattern. It is clear, therefore, that the seven seals are not included to represent an indeterminate number of obscurities.

Henceforth, it seems better to say that these seals are nothing but the will of God closing and opening the secret, when and how it pleases God's will, which, although it is one in itself, is considered multiple according to various effects, according to Ps 111:2: "Great are the works of the Lord, exquisite in all his purposes."[2] Therefore, the seven seals unveil the sevenfold distinctions of the revealed will of God in seven revelations, or what is to take place in seven periods.[3]

2. **And I saw** Here the difficulty of opening the seals is described, when it says: **And I saw a mighty angel** This seems to have been Gabriel who is interpreted as God's might. **"Who is worthy to open the scroll"** That is, to reveal the mystery of God. **"And break its seals?"** That is, to show how each seal proceeds from the divine will.

3. **And no one was able in heaven** The angels. **Or on the earth** Humans. **Or under the earth** The demons in whom the natural things remain intact. **To open the scroll** No one can understand the divine mysteries, unless God, who first revealed them to the human Christ and Christ to John, reveals them.

4. **And I began to weep bitterly** In this weeping John indicates the desire to know the future course of the Church.

5. **Then one** This infers the dignity of Christ, who alone was found worthy to receive these mysteries first and to announce them to others through John, when it is said: **Then one of the elders said to me,** By consoling me about my desire's fulfillment. Who this elder was is not said. Some say that he was Matthew, the evangelist, who spoke in the person of Christ (Mt 28:18), "All authority in heaven and on earth has been given to me"; therefore it is said: **"See, the Lion of the tribe of Judah has conquered,"** For Christ was the victor in his resurrection.

But whatever the truth, this argument does not seem

very strong, because John received this knowledge not from Matthew but by special revelation. Moreover, it was said earlier that the elders are understood to be the prelates of the Church. Therefore, it seems better to say that this elder was Peter, because it is said: **One** That is, the first among the Apostles in the same manner of speaking with which it is said in Gn 1:5, "And there was evening and there was morning, the first day." St. Peter had already passed over through martyrdom to glory, because he suffered under Nero. John, however, received this revelation after the time of Domitian. Thus the spirit of Peter assisting Christ or some image representing Peter said to John: **"Do not weep . . . , the Root of David,"** That is, descending from the root of David according to the flesh, as it was prophesied in Is 11, "A shoot shall come out from the stump of Jesse, and a branch shall grow out of his roots." **" . . . So that he can open the scroll"** To show the course of the Church preordained by God.

6. **Then I saw between the throne and the four living figures and among the elders a Lamb** That is, Christ in the middle of the churches established in his name throughout the world, as he himself says in Mt 28:20, "Lo I am with you always to the end of the age." Just as he was called the lion by virtue of his resurrection, so he is called the lamb by virtue of his sacrifice; there-fore it is also said: **Standing,** Because he was raised to eternal life, Rom 6:9: "Christ being raised from the dead will never die again." And **As if it had been slaughtered,** He is sacrificed daily in the Church, not by dying according to the flesh, because he was raised to eternal life, as has been said, but according to the effect and representation. In the oblation of the eucharist, the effect

of his passion is communicated to us. The same is also a representative likeness of it, according to which it is said in Lk 22:19: "Do this in remembrance of me." For that which represents something is called by its name, just as the image of Peter is called Peter, and for the same reason the Eucharist is called the sacrificed lamb to designate this. It is not said the lamb was simply slaughtered, but **As if slaughtered.**[4]

Having seven horns That is, powers. The same is indicated by **The seven spirits,** Because the seven gifts of the spirit are like seven horns or powers to reprimand the power of the enemy. . . .

7. **He went and took the scroll from the right hand of the one who was seated on the throne.** By this one should not understand that Christ received the knowledge of the course of the Church at that moment. The Spirit of Christ having been joined to the divinity from the instant of his creation knew all things that God knows by the knowledge of vision, including the course of the Church, as is clear from what has been said. Therefore, John's seeing him receive the scroll designates the reception of knowledge from the beginning of the creation of Christ's soul, but revealed anew to John and through him to the universal Church.

8. **When he had taken the scroll,** Here he describes the joy of those assisting Christ: first those assisting him in the Church militant; and second in the Church triumphant, at the place: **Then I looked, and I heard** (Rv 5:11). Concerning the first it is said: **When he had taken the scroll,** To reveal the progression of the Church. **The four living creatures** That is, the four patriarchates of the Church. **And the twenty-four elders** That is, the cathedrals of the

universal Church dispersed throughout the world, and through this others established by them are understood. **Fell before the Lamb,** For this they held the materials to venerate him. **Each holding a harp** Which is explained by what follows: **Which are the prayers** Metaphorically—and through these and through similes the method is revealed to explain the rest, as has been said above.

9. **They sing a new song:** That is, pertaining to the New Testament. **You are worthy . . .** The meaning is clear from what has been said above. **From every tribe . . .** The Church is gathered from all nations.

10. **You have made us to be a kingdom and priests serving our God.**[5] That is, participants of a kingdom. **And priests** The sacrifices of praise being offered to God. **And we will reign "above" the earth.** It is not said **"On" the earth** Where the saints are tread under foot, but **"Above" the earth.** That is, in heaven, where the saints rule with Christ.

11. **Then I looked,** Here he describes the joy of those assisting Christ in the Church triumphant: **Then I looked, and I heard the voice of many angels** In this, the greatest number of them is noted, according to Jb 25:3, "Is there any number to his armies?" And the same is designated in that which follows: **They numbered myriads of myriads and thousands of thousands . . .**

12. **"Worthy is the Lamb . . ."** All these things he held or more before the passion as I say, on account of the glory of the body and of that which followed. Therefore, this reception is accepted here for the manifestation of those things to the praise and the honor of the name of Christ. Consequently the praise of Christ is placed in all creatures when it is said: **And every creature which is in**

heaven The people who are already home. **And on the earth** The living still on the way. **And under the earth** For all creatures, animals, and things lacking life are called to praise Christ inasmuch as they are matter and have the occasion of praising him, because intellectual creatures ascend through them to understand God and, as a consequence, to praise and glorify him. The rest that follows is clear from what has been said.

Notes

1. This citation is from Sermon 33 (*PL* 76:1593).

2. The Vulgate is different from the NRSV here.

3. In the historical/sequential method the images in the seven seals represent consecutive and defined periods of history. The method differs from the Joachite tradition in the amount of history for which it finds referents in the Apocalypse.

4. Nicholas also seems to have written a treatise on the Eucharist, *De Sacramento Eucharistiae;* see Gosselin, "Bibliographical Survey," pp. 405–23 for a list of his works. It would be helpful to compare these and other passages from the *Literal Postill* with the treatise, since not all scholars agree that Nicholas is actually its author.

5. The Vulgate and the NRSV differ here.

Chapter 6
THE COURSE OF HISTORY REVEALED
FROM THE APOSTLES TO DIOCLETIAN

1. **Then I saw the Lamb open** After the mode of divine revelation now the course (*decursus*) of fulfillment is described under the opening of the seven seals, by which the book was called sealed. According to the seven seals it is divided into seven parts, which are clear in the text (*litera*). Therefore, in the first part it says: **Then I saw the Lamb open one of the seven seals,** Namely, the first, in that manner of speaking by which it is said in Gn 1 "And there was evening and there was morning, the first day." That is, the first, whence consequently it is said there, "And there was evening and there was morning, the second day," and thus up to the seventh in this manner. In this way, the opening of the second, the third, and up to the seventh seal is described.

And I heard one of the four living creatures That is, the first, for the same reason that it was said of the seals, and thus it is done for the other three creatures. According to those who say that the living creatures signify the four evangelists, this was Mark, designated in the image of a lion, which has been discussed above in chapter 4. But since this interpretation does not agree with the order of the evangelists, in which Matthew is placed first and Mark second, therefore, I said above in chapter 4 that the four living creatures designate the four patriarchates of the Church. Therefore, I have to say that the first living creature was the patriarch of the first patriarchate of the Church, namely Jerusalem, who was St. James, called the brother of the Lord, because he was similar to him. He died earlier by the sword under Nero, as is clear from Josephus in Book 20 of *The Antiquities.*[1] This revelation was made to John at the time of Domitian. **"Come and See!"** The course of the primitive Church.

2. **. . . . And there was a white horse!** Which, as some expositors say, indicates the Emperor Caligula,[2] who immediately succeeded Tiberius under whom Christ had suffered. He is designated by the white horse because he did not threaten the Christians but, to some extent, consoled them; he sent Pilate, who judged Christ unjustly, into exile, and similarly Herod, who had beheaded John and scorned Christ in the passion (Lk 23). Therefore, it is added: **And he came out conquering and to conquer.** The adversaries of Christ, as it has been said. This, however, does not seem to me to be fitly said. For Caligula was so perverse that he sent his statue throughout the world to be adored as a God. Because those living in Judaea refused to do this, he sent Petronius with an army into Judaea to set up this statue in the temple and to kill those who refused, as Josephus says in *The Antiquities* and *The Wars of the Jews.* Nevertheless, Petronius did not give the order, because Caligula died beforehand.[3]

In that time the apostles and other Christians were living in Jerusalem and in Judaea, and it is clear that Caligula did not console them—instead, he was cruel. The order had been given to the rest of the inhabitants of Judaea to adore him. Although he had sent Herod and Pilate into exile, this was not on account of Christ, but for totally other causes, as Josephus reports, which, for brevity, I omit.[4]

Similarly because it is added: **He came out conquering and to conquer.** It does not seem fitting that this apply to Caligula, because he was shamefully killed in Rome for his cruelties, his wife was pierced, and his only daughter was dashed against a wall. Therefore, others seem to say better, namely, that the white horse is understood as the band of apostles made white by their sanctity of life.[5] St. James, bishop of the Church in Jerusalem (as Jerome says in *The Lives of Illustrious Men*), is said to have used not woolen vestments but linen and therefore white.[6] It is probably possible to determine the same about the other apostles, whence Muhammad calls them whitewashed men.

The one sitting on that horse is understood to be Christ, the rider and leader of them, according to Rom 8:14, "For all who are led by the Spirit of God are children of God." According to this, the line should be interpreted: **And there was a white horse!** Namely, the council of the apostles. **And its rider** Namely, Christ. **Had a bow** That is, the preached word. . . .

3. **When he opened the second seal,** This is the second part, in which the status (*status*) of the Church from the time of Nero up to that of the Emperor Titus is described, when it is said: **I heard the second living creature** According to what was said before, this was the first patriarch of the church of Antioch, namely St. Peter, who first ruled that church, as is said in *The Lives of Illustrious Men*, and had already died through martyrdom.[7] He said: **"Come and see."** The status of the Church under Nero.

4. **And out came another horse, bright red;** That is, the Roman people, which is called red at the time of Nero because Nero killed many of the Romans out of cruelty— even his own mother and wife, and he is said to have killed his brother, sister, and even his teacher, Seneca. In

another way more properly **"red;"** because Nero caused the City of Rome to be burned for it to seem like the fire of ancient Troy. In such a fire, out of the mixture of smoke and fire the appearance of redness is caused.

Its rider Namely, Nero having the power. **Was permitted** That is, having been permitted by God. **To take** That is, to carry off. **Peace from the earth,** Because the populace was thrown into confusion throughout the Roman Empire due to his evil deeds. **So that people would slaughter one another;** As a result of Nero's perfidy and after he killed himself, Otho, Galba, and Vitellius wanted to usurp the office. Out of their mutual struggle many were killed. **And he was given a great sword.** That is, the power of killing Christians. He started the first persecution against the Church, that is, persecutions instigated by Roman emperors. The Church had endured persecution earlier by the Jews. Indeed, the severe commands of Caligula were not directed against the Church, but against the inhabitants of Judah, of whom comparatively few were Christian; nor was the order executed, and, therefore, the first persecution of the Church is attributed to Nero. Even Claudius, who was emperor between Caligula and Nero, is not reputed to have persecuted the Christians. Nero, however, killed the leaders of the Apostles, namely, Peter and Paul, and ordered many other Christians in Rome to be killed.

5. **When he opened the third seal,** Here is the third part in which the status of the Church under Titus is described, when it is said: **I heard the third living creature** That is, the first patriarch of the Church in Alexandria, St. Mark, as it is held in the *Lives of Illustrious Men.*[8] **And there was a black horse!** That is, the Roman army, which

is effectively called black, just as the sun is called hot. For the Roman army under Titus so afflicted the inhabitants of Jerusalem that they were blackened by famine and by other afflictions, as Josephus relates in the book of *The Wars of the Jews.*[9]

Its rider Titus ruling that army. **Held a pair of scales** That is, divine justice, which he pursued in the siege; for he proceeded out of the ordination of divine justice. The Roman army partly killed and partly captured the Jews, in punishment for the death of Christ, just as was clearly predicted in Lk 19:43: "Indeed the days will come upon you, when your enemies will set up ramparts around you and surround you. . . ." Nevertheless, this was not the intention of Titus and his army, who came against the Jews for another reason, namely, their rebellion against Roman rule (as is clear from Josephus in the book of *The Wars of the Jews*[10]). Therefore, it is said that he was holding the scales in his hand and not in his mind. The work of divine justice was executed in this way, by the hand the work is understood, because thus it is effected.

6. **And I heard what seemed to be a voice in the midst of the four living creatures,** That is, from the throne of God around which there were four living creatures, as has been said above in chapter 4, and this indicates that what Titus did against the Jews proceeded from divine ordination from whom punishment proceeds, according to Amos 3:6, "Does disaster befall a city, unless the Lord has done it?"

"Two pounds of wheat for a denarius,"[11] To understand this, one must know what Hugh of Fleury says about the end of the war of the Romans against the Jews. Weary of much slaughter, the Romans finally sought to whom they might sell slaves, but, because many slaves were found for sale but few buyers, those who were buying did not fail to obtain thirty slaves for one coin. Just as they had bought the Lord for thirty denarii, so conversely for one denarius thirty were bought.[12] Moreover, a coin and a denarius are one and the same, as the Lord says in Mt 22:19, "Show me the coin used for the tax." And it is added, "And they brought him a denarius." Moreover, it was called a denarius because it was worth ten ordinary coins. Similarly, *bilibris* (of two pounds) is a word composed of *bis* and *libra*, because it contains two pounds.

Indeed, here, five Jews are designated by one pound, because the five books of Moses are accepted by all the Jews. However, the Jews, who are called Sadducees, do not accept other books. Therefore, this is the sense of: **"Two pounds of wheat for a denarius, and three pounds of barley for a denarius,"** Just as from the cheaper Jews, who were for sale (who are designated by the barley which is a cheap grain), thirty were given for one denarius, as it has been said, so, from the stronger and more capable of serving, ten Jews were sold for one denarius.

"But do not damage the olive oil and the vine!" By the **"vine,"** that is, "joy," the Christians are understood, who were filled with spiritual joy, according to what is said in Acts 13:52, "And the disciples were filled with joy and with the Holy Spirit." And similarly the "oil" refers to the devotion and mutual charity, as it is said in Acts 4:34, "For as many as owned lands or houses sold them and brought the proceeds of what was sold, and laid them at the feet of the apostles, who distributed to each as any had need." These were not hurt by the army of Titus.

Having been warned by an angel before his arrival, the Christians living in Jerusalem and in Judaea had crossed beyond the Jordan to a city called Pella, ruled by Agrippa, who was allied with the Romans.

7. **When he opened the fourth seal,**[13] Here the fourth part begins describing the status of the Church at the time of Domitian, because he persecuted the Church and did many other evil things in the Roman Empire. Therefore it is said, **I heard the voice of the fourth living creature** That is, of the patriarchate or the Bishop of Constantinople, who was already dead, just as it has been said in the other three seals.

8. **And there was a pale green horse!** That is, the Roman people. Domitian killed a large part of the senators and sent a great number of other nobles into exile charging them with crimes so that he might take their goods. Therefore, the rest of Rome and others were in great fear lest it also happen to them. Fear, moreover, makes the exterior limbs pale, and especially the face. Thus, the Roman Empire at that time is signified by the pale horse. **Its rider's name** Namely, Emperor Domitian. **Was Death,** Actively and passively because he killed many innocents, as it has been said, especially Christians, whom he persecuted. Finally he was killed by the Roman Senate because of his cruelty, as it is reported in *The Legend of St. John The Evangelist.*[14] **And Hades followed with him;** Because after the course of this present life, he was immediately dragged off to the punishment of Gehenna. **He was given authority over a fourth of the earth,** In that he had enlarged the Roman Empire. **To kill with the sword,** Because in all these regions, many Christians had been killed by the sword in his hand.

Famine, Many who had died had been tortured by starvation in prisons. **And by the wild beasts of the earth.** Because many of them were handed over to be devoured by wild beasts, as is clear in the legends of many martyrs. Some were martyred in many other ways, namely, by hanging, drowning, and burning. **With pestilence,** As every method of afflicting the martyrs is included. From the above it is clear that just as in Zec 6 various horses in fourfold color designated four kingdoms, as it has been said in that place, so in this place the reign of Christ is designated by the white horse, just as it was among the twelve apostles and the first believers. The other three horses designate Roman rule, the status of which was different in three periods.

9. **When he opened the fifth seal,** Here the fifth part begins in which he describes the persecution of the Church from Emperor Trajan, who succeeded Domitian, to Diocletian. Trajan directed the third persecution of the Church; Marcus Aurelius, the fourth; Severus, the fifth; Maximinus, the sixth; Decius, the seventh; Valerian, the eighth; Aurelian, the ninth. Although there were many emperors between them, in whose reigns many Christians were martyred, these are especially known to have conducted persecutions of the Christians, because they made and renewed edicts against them. When some were martyred during other reigns, this was because of the edicts of their predecessors, which they did not renew. Therefore, in the times of the emperors noted above the altars of the churches were not fixed but set in secret places and especially in the crypts of the martyrs in which their bodies were buried, and a wooden altar was carried and erected for the celebration of mass.

When he opened the fifth seal, I saw under the altar the souls of those who had been slaughtered That is, the martyrs who were killed whose bodies were there. It is similar to the manner of speaking in Ex 1:5, "The total number of people born to Jacob." In other words, people. Their souls did not come from the thigh of Jacob, as if from a vine, but were infused by God through creation—their bodies were taken from Jacob through generation. **For the word of God** This refers to the teachers who were martyred because they preached the divine word. **And for the testimony** This refers to the simple Christians who were martyred because they refused to deny Christ, but protested, nonetheless, by believing in him.

10. **They cried out with a loud voice,** This cry is nothing other than the manifestation of the wickedness of the tyrants before God who deserve to be punished and of the innocence of the martyrs who deserve to be rewarded, just as the Lord himself declares to Cain in Gn 4:10, "Listen; your brother Abel's blood is crying out to me from the ground!" That is, his innocence proclaims that your wickedness needs to be punished in satisfaction for his death. Therefore it is added: **"How long, Lord?"** Make things right! You who are **"Holy and true. How long will it be before you judge and avenge our blood on the inhabitants of the earth?"** That is, on the ruling tyrants on the earth.

11. **They were each given a white robe** Because the glory of the soul was given to each. **And they were told to rest** Their bodies in the graves. **A little longer** That is, to the judgement, which is a little while compared to eternity; whereupon it is said in 1 Jn 2:18, "Children, it is the last hour!" They will rise in glorious bodies, and thus

they will have a second robe, which is the glory of the body. **Until the number would be complete.** . . . Afterwards many Christians were killed, and still more will be killed in the persecution of Antichrist.

12. **When he opened the sixth seal, I looked,** Here he describes the status of the Church under Diocletian, who caused the tenth persecution against the Church with his colleague, Maximian. This persecution was more vicious than the earlier ones, such that within thirty days he crowned 17,000 men and women with martyrdom. This is what John describes in the opening of the sixth seal. It is divided into two parts: first, the imminence of the persecution; second, the sweetness of the divine consolation, at the place: **After this** (Rv 7:1).

Concerning the first it is said: **And there came a great earthquake;** By order of Diocletian and Maximian, the judges and rulers killed Christians in all parts of the Roman Empire. **The sun** . . . , That is, Christ, who is the sun of justice, was denigrated; that is, his good name and also his body, that was impugned with the charge that they [his followers] were evildoers and magicians. For they were instructed by Christ through the apostles and the other disciples whom he had taught concerning the things the unbelievers called them. Thus, as he was in them, they denigrated the name of Christ. **The full moon became** . . . , Because then the whole Church was filled with the red blood of the martyrs.

13. **And the stars of the sky fell to the earth** That is, many leaders in the Church in fear of death apostatized—Pope Marcellinus in fear of death sacrificed to the idols, and because of this one can conclude that many others did the same. Nevertheless, St. Marcellinus

repented and became a martyr for Christ; the see of Rome ceased for 7½ years because of this threatening persecution.

14. **The sky vanished as a scroll** Here the sky represents the Church of the present time as in Mt 13:44, "The kingdom of heaven is like treasure hidden in a field." As Gregory explains in Homily 37, Christians were hiding themselves insofar as they were able, except a few who out of fervor offered themselves for martyrdom.[15] **And every mountain** The Christians were sought out and killed on remote mountains and cliffs and the islands of the sea where they were hidden. These places are said to move because the inhabitants moved, just as it is said of Paris that it does or experiences what its people do or experience.[16]

15. **Then the kings** In all of these parts of the world the Catholic faith had already spread to persons from every station in life—some believed, who, not enduring the rage of the persecution of Diocletian and Maximian, sought to hide themselves in the caves under the mountains. Therefore it is added: **Hid** Some of them fearing to be captured there and to be put to death by prolonged torture desired to die more quickly, lest during the torture they would be inclined to deny Christ. And this desire is expressed, when it is said:

16. **Calling to the mountains and rocks, "Fall on us and hide us from the face of the one seated . . ."** Of the one angered against us, although anger does not properly occur in God; nevertheless, he is said to be angry against some metaphorically, when he punishes them, because he conducts himself according to the manner of anger. When he punishes the elect, however, he does it more out of

kindness to increase their merits and rewards. **"And from the wrath of the Lamb;"** That is, of the human Christ, who was seen to be angry against his Church in a manner of speaking.

17. **"For the great day of their wrath has come"** That is, the time of the great persecution permitted by God. **"And who is able to stand?"** As if to say a very few, because Pope Marcellinus, who was the head of the Church, fell, as it was said above; therefore, it seemed difficult that other lesser ones could stand.

Moreover it is explained by others thus: **Calling on the mountains** By the mountains and rocks the saints are understood, who were in that country, and are called mountains because of their exaltation to heaven, and rocks because they were firm in their goodness; the faithful requested their prayers in the midst of persecution. And this is the sense: **And they call to the mountains,** That is, to the saints. **"Fall upon us"** That is, condescend to us. **"And hide us from the face of the one seated"** That is, protect us by your prayers against God and the Lamb, so that the rage of this persecution may cease. But the other exposition seems more literal.

Notes

1. *Jewish Antiquities*, Bk. 20, Chap. 9. Josephus is edited and translated in 9 vols. by H. St. J. Thackeray in the Loeb Classical Library (Cambridge, Mass.: Harvard University Press, 1966–69).

2. See Alexander, for example, p. 91.

3. Josephus, *Antiquities*, Bk. 19, Chap. 6.

4. Josephus, *Antiquities*, Bk. 18, Chap. 4.

5. Here Nicholas appears to choose Peter's interpretation (p. 463) over that of Alexander (p. 91). He had both commentaries at hand as he wrote this continuous commentary.

6. *De Viris illustribus* (*PL* 25:829).

7. Ibid., p. 827.

8. Ibid., p. 843.

9. Josephus, *The Jewish War*, Bk. 5, Chap. 10, Loeb Classical Library, vol. 3, ed. H. St. J. Thackeray (1968).

10. Ibid., 2.

11. The NRSV translates "A quart of wheat for a day's pay, and three quarts of barley for a day's pay."

12. See Alexander, p. 96, and Peter, p. 466—Both cite Josephus.

13. The Antwerp edition has a textual error here calling it the fifth seal ("quintum") instead of the fourth.

14. Nicholas may have this story through Isidore of Seville or James of Voragine, author of the *Golden Legend*.

15. Possibly Sermon 35.

16. This is one of the few references to Paris in the *Literal Postill* and has served as an important biographical source for Nicholas.

Chapter 7
THE CONSOLATION OF THE CHURCH
UNDER CONSTANTINE

1. **After this I saw** After the description of bitter persecutions, he describes the sweet consolation that occurred in the Church of God at the time of Helen's son, Constantine. It is divided into two parts: first this consolation of the Church militant; and second those existing in the Church triumphant, at the place: **After this I looked, and there was a great multitude** (Rv 7:9).

The first is also in two parts, because, first, the brevity of the persecutions is promised, namely, of the four tyrants ruling in the diverse parts of the Roman Empire; second their repression by Constantine is promised, at the place: **I saw another angel** (Rv 7:2).

Concerning the first, one should know, as it is said in Book 9 of *Church History*, that after Diocletian and Maximian retired their imperial insignia they established two emperors, namely, Galerius and Constantius. Galerius instituted two caesars, namely, Severus in Italy and Maximin in the East. Constantius and Helen bore a son by the name of Constantine, who, upon the death of his father, was made emperor and joined in a consortium of the empire with Licinius, who, although he was at first a friend of the Christians, afterwards became a persecutor.[1]

Maxentius was a tyrant at Rome, and thus there were four persecutors of the Church in four parts of the Empire: Maximin in the East, Severus in Italy, Maxentius in Rome, and Licinius in Alexandria, which is in Egypt. Likewise it should be noted that in this book rulers, in particular, and dignitaries are frequently called angels, just as it was said in chapter 1 about the seven bishops of the churches who are called angels. If they are good angels, they are angels of God; if they are evil angels, they are angels of Satan—especially for the time they are evil, just as it was said above in chapter 3 about the angel of Sardis,[2] **"You have a name of being alive, but you are dead."** (3:1) Therefore, in this manner, here the four persecutors of the Church are called angels, when it is said: **After this I saw four angels standing** That is, rulers. **At the four corners of the earth,** That is, the four parts of the empire, as has been said. **Holding back the four winds of the earth** That is, impeding the doctors of the Church from preaching the word of God, about which it was said in Song 4:16 "Awake, O north wind, and come, O south wind! Blow upon my garden that its fragrance may be wafted abroad:" Because through the breath of preaching the garden of the Church militant is made fertile. **On earth** Some Christians were living in the desert, some on islands in the sea, others were fleeing the persecution into the forests; all of these are designated by the names of these places just as the Parisian inhabitants are called by its name so that it is commonly said that Paris observed such a feast, however, meaning the people living there.[3]

2. **I saw** Here he describes the repression of the four tyrants. First the act of repression is described; second the result is added, at the place: **And I heard** (7:4). Concerning the first, he sets forth the condition of the restraining, when it is said: **And I saw another angel** That is, the Emperor Constantine. **Ascending from the rising of the Sun,** By the order of Christ, who is the sun of justice, he ascended to the imperial rank to give peace

to the Church. **Having the seal** That is, the sign of the cross of Christ. For it is written in the *Church History 9, 9* that, as Constantine was coming to Rome against Maxentius, who was tyrannizing the city, he thought frequently about the disposition of the war and prevailed upon the God of heaven for victory, although he was not yet baptized. Gazing into the sky, he saw the sign of the cross glowing red, and, as he marvelled at the unusual vision, he saw angels assisting and saying to him, "In this sign you will conquer." Thus secure about the future victory, just as he had seen the sign of the cross, he ordered it depicted on the military standards and proceeded against Maxentius and obtained a complete triumph.[4]

And he called with a loud voice to the four angels That is, the four tyrants noted above. **Who had been given power** That is, it was permitted. **To damage earth and sea,** The Christians inhabiting desert land and islands,

3. **Saying, "Do not damage"** He restrained the four tyrants from harming the Christians—some by waging war, as it was said about Maxentius. Similarly, he restrained Licinius, who was cruelly persecuting Christians in Alexandria and Egypt, and the two others he deterred by his decree, as it is held in *Church History,* Book 9.[5] **"Until we have marked"** Constantine baptized by Sylvester honored and exalted the Church and especially the priests and other ministers of the Church and gave the Christians many privileges. Thus by word and example he led many to be baptized, and through the ministry of Christian priests he sealed his servants.

4. **And I heard** Here he describes the result of this restraint, which is the multiplication of the believers in Christ. The expositors say that here first the number of the

converts to Christ from Judaism is noted, and thus he adds **Out of every tribe . . .** Afterwards, he adds: **After this I looked,** (7:9). Here he includes the many converts from the Gentiles—a vastly greater number than from Judaism. I submit myself to better judgement, but the former does not seem reasonable, because even before the time of Constantine the Jews were obstinate in their infidelity; therefore, it does not seem possible that at the time of Constantine many were baptized, as it is said here: 144,000. Likewise, out of every tribe, except Dan, who was replaced by Joseph, 12,000 are said to be sealed; nevertheless, according to the Hebrews and the Latins, ten of the tribes were captured and held beyond the Caspian Mountains.[6] Thus, none of these could have been baptized.

Similarly, the latter point concerning the conversion of the Gentiles does not seem probable, because the text differs in many ways, which will be clearer as we proceed. Therefore, (as it seems to me at present)[7] in this first part (7:4–8), the multitude of converts to Christ at the time of Constantine from whatever tribe or nation describes those who in baptism follow the real name, Israel, as Isaiah foretold in chapter 44:3ff., "I will pour my spirit upon your descendants, and my blessing on your offspring. They shall spring up. . . . This one will say, 'I am the Lord's,' another will be called by the name of Jacob, yet another will write on the hand,'The Lord's,' and adopt the name of Israel." This refers to the Gentile conversion to Christ, just as it was discussed more fully there.

The Apostle also says this in Rom 2, "For a person is not a Jew who is one outwardly, nor is true circumcision something external and physical. Rather, a person is a Jew who is one inwardly," namely through faith in Christ, "And real circumcision is a matter of the heart," namely, through the rejection of vices. Thus it is clear that the name "Israel," according to substance and truth, transferred to the regenerated people in Christ. As a consequence, the names of the twelve tribes of Israel transferred to the twelve apostles of the New Testament, who correspond to the twelve patriarchs of the Old Testament. The tribe of Dan is omitted, because from him it is said Antichrist will be born.[8]

5–8. It should also be known that, when it is said here: **Twelve thousand were sealed,** A determinate number is used for an indeterminate; for in those days many more were baptized throughout the world, just as it was said earlier in the fourth chapter that the twenty-four elders refer to all of the prelates of the Church, which is a much greater number, as it was said there.[9] These things having been said, the text is clear.

9. **After this I looked,** Here he describes the consolation of those in the Church triumphant. Even as after the bitter persecution in the times of Diocletian and Maximian, a great consolation in the Church militant was established by the Constantinian peace, so a great joy was established by Christ for the souls of the martyrs at that time in the Church triumphant. Therefore, he describes this joy first; second, John is instructed more about these things: **Then one of the elders addressed me, . . .** (7:13).

Concerning the first he says: **After this I looked, and there was a great multitude** Of martyrs. **That no one could count,** Diocletian and Maximian martyred so many that a specific number was not humanly possible to count; for within thirty days 17,000 were said to be martyred. On one day, in particular, Maximian killed the legion of Thebes, in which there were 6,067 Christian soldiers.[10] By their command, judges in many regions killed so many Christians that it was beyond reckoning; for Diocletian is said to have ruled for twenty years. **From every nation, from all tribes and peoples and languages,** It seems that this does not deal with the Gentile conversions, as some say, but with those having been martyred by Diocletian and Maximian, among whom there were some who had converted form Judaism to Christ and from every people and race. **Standing before the throne** The clear vision of God. **And before the Lamb,** Because just as the blessed are fed internally in the sight of God, so also they are fed externally in the sight of the humanity of Christ, as St. Augustine says on John.[11]

Robed in white, By the glory of the soul that the white stole designates, as was said in the previous chapter. **With palm branches in their hands.** In a sign of perfect victory, not possessed in the present life, in which all, inasmuch as they are saints, are always in battle. Thus it seems, this does not refer to the baptized on the way, but the martyrs in heaven.

10. **They cried with a loud voice,** For in heaven the praise of God is continuous. **Saying, "Salvation . . ."** That is, the salvation which we have that is in us from God and the Lamb.

11. **And all the angels stood around the throne** As if ready to execute the will of God. **And around the elders and the four living creatures,** That is, of the bishops and of the patriarchs already ruling in heaven. **And they fell on their faces** Giving thanks to God for the triumph of the martyrs.

12. **Saying "Amen!"** After the praise of the martyrs mentioned above. **"Salvation belongs to our God"** (7:10) And their praise is added when it is said: **"Blessing"** That is, praise. **"And glory"** That is, the publication of the name etc. **"Be to our God forever and ever!"** One should not understand that something accrues to God in himself from creatures, but only in his effects.

13. **Then one of the elders addressed** Here John is instructed more fully concerning the martyrs, when it is said: **Then one addressed** According to those who say that the preceding text speaks about the conversions of the Gentiles at the time of Constantine, this elder was St. Sylvester. This, however, does not seem to be suitable, because St. Sylvester did not instruct John; he was born much later and flourished at the time of Constantine, who began to rule in the year 319. Therefore, it would seem that this elder was St. Peter, who is called one elder; that is, the first among the prelates of the Church, as has been said above in chapter 5.[12]

"Who are these robed in white?" That is, "You ought to know."

14. **I said to him, "Sir, you are the one"** "You who rule in the age with them." For before the revelation was made to John, Peter was transferred by martyrdom to glory, as was shown above in chapter 5. John says, therefore, "You who know, are able to speak concerning these things."

And he said to me, "These are they who have come . . ." Coming out from the world by martyrdom at the time of the emperors, Diocletian and Maximian; that was the time of the greatest tribulation, as has been said. This adds to the argument that this text does not address the conversions to faith at the time of Constantine, because at that time the Church was not in tribulation but in the greatest consolation; therefore, as I have said, it refers to the martyrs in the preceding times.

Therefore it is added: **"They have washed their robes and made them white in the blood . . ."** Their blood was poured out, and therefore it is rightly called the blood of the Lamb; it is the blood of his members in which he said that he experienced persecution, Acts 9:4, "Saul, Saul, why do you persecute me?" Moreover, the martyrs received the first stole, that is, the glory of the soul, as it has been said above by the pouring of their blood.

15. **"For this reason they are before the throne of God,"** Seeing him face to face. **"And worship him day and night"** Because there is continuous praise! (Ps 83, "Happy are those who live in your house, ever singing your praise").[13] **"And the one who is seated . . ."** God. **"Will shelter them."** Because they are not able to be torn from him.

16. **"They will hunger no more"** That is, they will experience no more tribulation or inquietude, because the appetite will be quieted in beatitude.

17. **"For the Lamb at the center of the throne"** Namely, Christ. **"Will be their shepherd,"** Without interference; moreover, he rules the faithful living on earth through the Church's ministers. **"And he will guide them to springs of the water of life,"** By sustaining the soul's glory in them until they receive the glory of the body in the future resurrection, when they will be in the springs of the water of life in a twofold glory of body and soul. **"And God will wipe away every tear from their**

eyes." They will no longer have any material sadness but will have the full and perfect consolation.

It is possible to argue against my exposition of the text: first, because it is said: **"After this I looked, and there was a great multitude"** (7:9) With the result that it does not seem to speak about the martyrs at the time of Constantine's predecessors, which he had discussed earlier, but rather the conversions of the Gentiles at his own time, as some expositors say. Second, because in chapter 21 speaking about the heavenly city John says: **And I saw no temple in it.**[14] (21:22). He seems to be speaking not about martyrs already in heaven but about the faithful who are still on the way.

To the first it must be said that when it is said: **"After this I looked, etc."** The word "after" refers not to the order of events[15] but to the order of vision or description. Those things which happen earlier are frequently shown and described later in prophecy, as it is clear in the Old and New Testaments; therefore it is not an effective argument.[16]

To the second point one should say that immediately after this verse (21:22) it is added: **For its temple is the Lord God the Almighty and the Lamb.** Therefore, it is clear that, through this word of John, the Temple is not excluded from the heavenly city in any way, but only the material and figurative temple, such as was in the Old Testament with respect to the New and in the New with respect to the heavenly. The worship of God in the New Testament is a certain figure and representation of the worship itself or the praise of the holy angels and the blessed in heaven. The heavenly worship does not point to anything, and therefore it is in no way a figure, because there God is worshiped and praised as a clear and present vision without a figure or enigma, and there the figurative temple is denied. The Lord omnipotent is called its temple; just as it will be more clearly shown when we will be there, God willing.[17]

Notes

1. Eusebius, *Church History*, either the end of Book 8 or the beginning of 9.

2. This is one of Nicholas's many hermeneutical rules in the commentary by which he will criticize his sources.

3. This is another reference to Paris. At the time he was writing the Apocalypse Commentary Nicholas was the administrator of the Franciscan Chapter of Burgundy, but he resided at the House of the Cordeliers in Paris.

4. Eusebius, *Church History*, 9, 9.7.

5. Ibid., Book 9.

6. Actually the Caucasus mountains near the Caspian Sea; this legend is a commonplace in the tradition, which Nicholas has in part carried over from Alexander, p. 117.

7. There is evidence in the commentary that Nicholas changed his mind about various interpretations over time. This is especially true in later passages that his models refer to the Franciscans and controversial historical events.

8. See Gregory the Great's *Moralia,* Book 31, 24 (*PL* 76:596).

9. This is another of Nicholas's rules for interpretation—an adaptation of Tyconius's hermeneutical rules which Nicholas

discusses in the second of the three famous prologues to the *Literal Postill.* The prologues can be found in *PL* 113.

10. For this legend see Robert M. Grant, *Augustus to Constantine: The Rise and Triumph of Christianity in the Roman World* (New York: Harper and Row, 1970), p. 226.

11. This source could not be located.

12. An example of Nicholas's rule of contemporaries.

13. Ps 84:4 in the NRSV.

14. The Antwerp edition omits the "non" from the citation from Rv 21:22.

15. "ad ordinem rei gestae"

16. This is another rule that Nicholas will use throughout the commentary. Nicholas does not see that earlier events in prophecy reported later in visions would seem to make more sense in a recapitulative method than in the historical/sequential.

17. This style may be an indication that Nicholas is thinking of a series of classroom lectures on Rv as he is writing.

Chapter 8
THE HERETICS: FROM ARIUS TO EUTYCHES

1. **When the Lamb opened the seventh seal,** Having described the battle of the Church in the preceding six seals, here in the opening of the seventh seal the battle of the Church against the heretics is described. This division, however, is not precise, because from the time of the

---

apostles heretics rose up against the Church, as is clear in the letters of the apostles, and after the time of Constantine there were and will be tyrants, but this distinction is accepted according to that principle that was described earlier.[1] Indeed heretics will be among the Christians to the end of the world, as the Savior demonstrated in Mt 13 with the parable of the weeds sown in the middle of the wheat, which he did not wish to be gathered until the harvest, meaning the time of judgement. As a result, this part in general lasts to the end or the end of this book.

It is divided into three parts; the first describes the status (*status*) of the Church preceding the judgement; the second, the status at the time of the judgement at the 19th chapter at the place: **Then I saw a great white throne**[2] The third, following at the place: **And I, John, saw the holy city** (21:2).

The first part is divided in two parts. The first describes the battle between the Church and heretics properly defined; the second between the Church and heretics by extension of the term (chapter 12). The first is yet divided in two parts. The first concerns the inventors of the heresies; the second their followers in the following chapter. The first is again in two parts, because first it continues what was being discussed; and second it follows with the heretics, at the place: **And the seven angels** (8:6).

In the preceding section there are two things said concerning the status of the Church, namely, the persecution of the tyrants and the following consolation by Constantine. Therefore at first, the first part is continued. Afterwards the second, at the place: **And the angel** (8:3).

First, he describes a brief persecution after the time of Constantine administered by Julian the Apostate, who killed Paul and John and many others,[3] and he inflicted many evil and damnable things on the Christians, concerning whom it is said here: **There was silence in heaven for about half an hour.** That is, in the Church militant, which is frequently called heaven in this book, as has been said before. This Julian ordered churches to be closed, prohibited the divine office from being solemnly celebrated, and, thus, there was silence in heaven; nevertheless, because Julian the Apostate ruled briefly, namely, one year and six months, according to Jerome, therefore it is added: **For about half an hour.** After he was killed in the war with the Persians, the churches were opened and the Christian religion began to rejoice, according to the legends of the saints and martyrs, John and Paul.[4] The account continues, when it says,

2. **And I saw the seven angels** These seven angels and their trumpets are addressed one by one.

3. **Another angel** This is the continuation of the second part of the preceding section—the liberation of the Church through Constantine followed by the building of churches and the celebration of the divine rites.[5] Pope Damasus added to this celebration by ordering that psalms be sung day and night in the churches and that at the end of the psalms it be said, "Glory to the Father and to the Son etc." **Another angel** Namely, Pope Damasus, who was not one of the seven noted above. **Came and stood at the altar;** Because he presided over the Church of Rome. **Holding a golden censer** That is, a heart devoted to God, according to Ps 141:2, "Let my prayer be counted

as incense before you." **He was given a great quantity of incense** These are the prayers of the saints; for through the apostolic authority given by God himself, the prayers of the saints are increased and multiplied throughout the world. **To offer with the prayers of all the saints** It is the duty of the highest pontiff to bear the devotion of the people to God, since he is the head of the universal Church.

5. **Then the angel took the censer . . . and threw it from the altar.** Out of the fervor for charity he received from God, he led the inhabitants of the earth in fervent devotion, as it is said: **And there were peals of thunder,** Of holy preaching. **Rumblings,** Of divine praise. **And flashes of lightening,** Of shining miracles. For at that time many of the prelates and the devout possessed the grace to perform miracles in the Church. **And an earthquake.** By these earthly hearts were moved to do the good. Consequently the continuation depends on the following when it is said:

6. **Now the seven angels . . .** Who are discussed now.

7. **The first angel** Here the heresiarchs are discussed. Although there were many, only four receive express mention against whom the general and principal councils had convened. It is divided into four parts, as we will see. In the first Arius is mentioned, who, inflated by pride, asserted the error over against the doctrine of the Holy Trinity, saying that just as the Father and the Son and the Holy Spirit are distinct in person, so also they are distinct in essence. Thus, only the Father is true God; the Son and the Holy Spirit are creatures, and neither is able to be called God, except by participation.

Against this error a general council of 318 bishops

assembled in the city of Nicea in Bithynia, and there the perverse dogma of Arius was condemned. Nevertheless, his many followers did not abandon the error but renewed it, infected many leaders and emperors, and persecuted the catholics, as will be shown in the following. Therefore, Arius is addressed by this angel. **And the first angel** That is, Arius. For all good or evil persons in this book are called angels, as I said in chapter 1. **Blew his trumpet,** He proclaimed the heresy with great bellowing and with pride. **And there came hail and fire, mixed with blood,** That is, a great storm, which is frequently and commonly called hail in the Church, which because of this heresy was divided within itself, as it is said in the 10th Book of *Church History.*[6] This storm made the face of the Church ugly and quite disgraceful; for it was not devastated from the outside as earlier, but from its own; the one drove into exile; the other was driven away, and it was said that both were from the Church. **And fire . . . ;** That is, the fire of imitation, on account of which blood followed, and especially at the time of the Emperor Valens, who having lapsed into the Arian heresy, persecuted the catholics by burning some of them and killing others by the sword and afflicting others by various methods.

And a third of the earth . . . , This third part of the earth is the Christian; the other two parts are the Jewish, and the pagan who did not have the law of Moses; nor did they accept the faith of Christ. Therefore, John speaks here about the third part (which is called Christianity), whose laity were corrupted by the fire of evil Arianism called the earth, because they were attentive to earthly deeds. The prelates and the clergy are signified by the trees, because by their understanding of the Scriptures they were elevated above the laity. The green grass refers to those newly converted to Christianity—the Goths—who, wishing to become Christians, sent to Emperor Valens for Christian priests who would teach them the catholic faith and the Church's sacraments. He sent them Arian presbyters, as he himself was Arian, who misled them into the Arian heresy.[7] Therefore, it is said: **And a third part of the earth was burned up,** As the text makes it clear.

8. **The second angel** This addresses the second heresiarch, namely, Macedonius, who differed from Arius, saying that the Son was of the same nature with the Father, but he agreed with him saying that the Holy Spirit was a creature and a servant of the Son. Therefore, about him it is said: **The second angel** That is, Macedonius, who is called the angel of Satan. **Blew his trumpet,** That is, moved by arrogant pride he taught the error. **Like a great mountain,** That is, a great heresy. **Burning with fire,** Namely, of treachery. **Was thrown into the sea.** That is, into the Church, the "sea" used because of baptism; the sea is the receptacle of all water, and the Church is a receptacle through the sacrament of baptism.

9. **A third of the sea became blood,** That is, the third part of the baptismal water is defiled, taking it in a broad sense. Baptism is conferred in the name of the Trinity; the third person is the Holy Spirit, who, according to the error of Macedonius, is said to be defiled, since he asserted that he is a creature of a servile condition, as has been said. **A third of the living creatures in the sea died,** In that error many who were regenerated and made new creatures by baptism were misled by the error of Macedonius. **And a third of the ships were destroyed.** The greatest part of

the prelates and curates through whom others should be led to the gate of salvation were misled through this error. Against Macedonius the second universal synod of 150 bishops was gathered to condemn this error.[8]

10. **The third angel** This addresses the third heresiarch, namely Pelagius, who at the time of the emperors Arcadius and Honorius erred concerning the grace of the Holy Spirit asserting that without it a person was able to merit eternal life by pure natural abilities. He also said that children are born without original sin and that they are not purged from sin by the baptismal water. About this, therefore, it is said: **The third angel** That is, Pelagius. **Blew his trumpet,** It is explained as above. **And a great star fell from heaven,** That is, from the Church militant, which is frequently called heaven in the New Testament, as has been said above. Pelagius fell from this heaven into this error, and it follows: **A great star** For he was a literate and religious man, namely, a monk. **Blazing like a torch,** He misled many by his erudition and by the appearance of sanctity in religious habit and conversation. **And it fell on a third part of the rivers. . . .** The springs and rivers indicate the Church gathered and sanctified by the waters of baptism.

11. **The name of the star is Wormwood.** Because he was preaching against the sweetness of the grace of the Holy Spirit. **A third of the waters became wormwood,** Because a great part of the Church was misled by his perverse dogma. **And many died from the water,** Spiritually. **From the water,** That is, from his perverse teachings. **Because it was made bitter.** That is, contrary to the life-giving spiritual sweetness of the Holy Spirit.

12. **The fourth angel** This addresses the fourth

heresiarch, namely Eutyches, who asserted that there was one nature in our Lord Jesus Christ, just as there was one person. He said that out of the divine and human nature in the incarnation one nature was made by a certain confusion or commixture, just as a unique nature results out of a mixture of elements. But this is impossible, since the divine nature does not mix with another, nor is it in any way transmutable. Therefore, about him it is said: **The fourth angel** Namely, Eutyches. **Blew his trumpet,** It is explained as above. **And a third of the sun** That is, of the deity, which is called the sun in Wis 5:6, "And the sun of understanding did not shine on us." Moreover, this part is accepted generally, inasmuch as the Son is one of the three persons in the Godhead, who, according to the error of Eutyches, is said to have been marred, because, according to him, he was neither man nor God, just as a mixture is none of the elements but another nature resulting from them.

And a third of the moon, That is, of the Church, whose many naive people were infected and damaged by this error. **And a third of the stars,** That is, of the bishops, some of whom agreed and subscribed to Eutyches and thus were blinded by the shades of the error. **A third of the day was kept from shining, and likewise the night.** By the day the New Testament is understood and by the night, the Old. "The night is far gone, the day is near" (Rom 13:12). This therefore is the sense (*sensus*), that this Eutyches and his followers obscured the Old and New Testaments, which speak concerning the divine and human nature of Christ; for example, concerning the distinct and unconfused in Christ which he expounded perversely.

13. **Then I looked,**[9] After John spoke about the inventors of the heresies, here he speaks concerning their followers. First he begins with a brief preface; second he continues with the intention in the following chapter. Concerning this he says: **And I looked and I heard an eagle crying with a loud voice** That is, of himself, John, who is designated by an eagle. For he speaks concerning himself as if of another person, as he commonly does in his Gospel where in the last chapter he says about himself, "This is the disciple who is testifying to these things. . . ."

Notes

1. See previous passage concerning "ad ordinem rei gestae."

2. Actually 20:11.

3. See Alexander (p. 123), who combined Frutolf-Ekkehard 114, 34–35, and 115, 8–9; and see *Sächsische Weltchronik* 125, 31–32 and 126, 4–5.

4. I have not been able to locate this source.

5. In other words, the beginning of chapter 8 continues the events of chapter 7 before it moves to the theme of the heretics.

6. A discussion of Arius is not in Book 10 of Eusebius's *Church History*, but Peter Auriol has a lengthy discussion of Arius at this point, p. 476.

7. Alexander, p. 129, who cited Frutolf-Ekkehard 119, 48–49.

8. Constantinople in 381.

9. At the opening of chapter 8 Lyra notes this verse as the second part of the discussion of the heretics.

Chapter 9
THE FOLLOWERS OF THE HERETICS:
THE VANDALS, THE ITALIANS, AND THE GOTHS

1. **And the fifth angel** Here St. John proceeds with the followers of the heresies, who are properly called heretics. And it is divided into three parts, because first it addresses the Vandals, who are properly called heretics; second the Italians, at the place: **And the sixth angel** (9:13); and third the Goths in the 11th chapter, at the place: **And in that hour** (11:13). The first part is divided in two, because first John delivers the theme; and second he explains it in a manner of speech, at the place: **In appearance** (9:7). Concerning the first, it should be noted that Emperor Valens sent Arian priests to the Goths, who wanted to receive the faith of Christ, by whom they were infected with the Arian heresy, and similarly to the Vandals, who caused great tribulation in Africa, in Italy, and also in Gaul, as it is reported in Book 21 of the *Speculum historialis* and in many chronicles.[1] It is said, therefore: **And the fifth angel** That is, Valens, who began to rule in the year 367.

And I saw a star that had fallen from heaven to earth, That is, Valentinian, who, persuaded by his wife, fell from the height of the catholic faith into the Arian heresy,[2] who is called an angel here and a star, as was said in chapter 1 that the same persons are called stars and angels. "The seven stars are the angels of the seven churches" (1:20). **And he was given the key;** That is, the power to reveal and to exalt the condemned heresy of Arius. By imperial power he sent Arian priests to infect many peoples; therefore, it is added:

2. **. . . From the shaft rose smoke . . .** That is, an erroneous teaching; therefore, it is added: **And the sun . . . was darkened** That is, Christ, who according to that heresy, was denied to be true God, as has been said in the preceding chapter. **And the air** That is, the Church, which is illumined by Christ just as the air by the visible sun. Moreover, in these times the Church was obscured by the error of Arius to such an extent that the greater part of the Church became Arian.

3. **Then from the smoke came locusts . . . ,** The Vandals, who are called locusts, were infected by the Arian heresy, because just as locusts jump from place to place, so the Vandals crossed from Spain to Africa and then invaded Italy and Gaul, devastating them. Therefore it is added: **And they were given authority** Namely, of harming people by securities, deceptions, and weapons. This God permitted them in secret judgement.

4. **They were told** That is, having been foretold by God. **Not to damage . . .** It should be known that before the invasion of the Vandals, Africa was inhabited partly by Christians and partly by pagans, as was true of many lands at the time. Moreover, they killed the pagans, not the Christians, and these Christians are signified by the lesser: **The grass of the earth** The ordinary: **Any green growth,** And the greater: **The Trees.**

They were told not to damage . . . , but only those people That is, the pagans who were not sealed by the sign of the cross. **They were told** This refers to the

Christians concerning whom this had been foretold. For in one context of a text, Holy Scripture sometimes crosses from some persons to others by speaking as if they were the same, as is clear in Ps 78:34, "When he killed them, they sought him." It is certain here that some were killed while others sought him to repent.[3] In the same way, John speaks here about the inhabitants of Africa, who were in part Christian and in part pagan, and in the same context it crosses from one to the other.

5. **They were allowed to torture them** Although they did not kill the Christians, as has been said, nevertheless, they afflicted them in many ways, especially by expelling the bishops and the doctors and by torturing them physically. Huneric, king of the Vandals, sent many bishops into exile, and similarly Thrasamund, who ruled after him, and Gaiseric, who had the tongues of some orthodox bishops pulled out and completely amputated; they, nevertheless, spoke and preached by the gift of God, according to Gregory in *The Dialogues*, 4, 51.[4] **For five months,** This designates that the reign of the Vandals lasted for a period of five kings, and then it was ended by Belisarius, the patrician, who was sent by the Emperor Justinian to Africa. **And their torture ...** At first some of the kings simulated kindness to the Christians but later afflicted them to such an extent that many wished to die rather than to see such trampling of the church and its ministers, as it is said in 1 Mc 3:59, "It is better for us to die in battle than to see the misfortunes of our nation and of our sanctuary." Therefore it is added: **And in those days people will seek death. . . .** (9:6)

7. **In appearance** Here he uses a certain manner of speech, because he had called the Vandals locusts.

Therefore, he expresses the conditions of some Vandals with the term *locusts*. **In appearance the locusts were like horses equipped for battle.** Here indicating that the Vandals were warlike people. **On their heads** Gold in the Scripture signifies the brightness of wisdom. Among the rest of the barbarians the Vandals seemed to have more of the brightness of natural industry. . . .[5] **Their faces were like human faces,** Because reason, which distinguishes humans from the rest of animals, flourished more in them than the rest of the barbarian nations, as it was said: **Their hair like women's hair,** Because they valued being hairy, as it is among some peoples. **And their teeth like lions' teeth;** This indicates their ferocity.

9. **They had scales like iron breastplates,** They were armed to fight against other peoples. **And the noise of their wings was like the noise of many chariots** With great noise their army proceeded through Italy and Gaul, as has been said.

10. **They have tails** The meaning is clear from what has been said before.

11. **They have as a king over them** To understand this one should know that according to Dionysius, the natural qualities of the demons remained intact and consequently the distinct ranks remain among them. Moreover, it is held by the doctors that some fell from each rank, and thus the name of each and every demon remains. The first order of the lower hierarchy is called the order of rulers, because they command the diverse kingdoms. Just as the holy angels cause the diverse kingdoms to commit themselves to the good, so, in the opposite way, the evil angels compel them to evil. Here the evil angel commanding the Kingdom of the Vandals is discussed: **They have as king**

over them the angel of the bottomless pit; Compelling them to the destruction of the good; therefore, it is added: **His name in Hebrew is Abaddon,** That is, scattering and destroying. Here the name is put in the three principal languages, because many people from these languages were destroyed, or because John was writing to the universal Church, which was established in every language and signified by these.[6]

12. **The first woe is passed.** That is, one serious persecution, namely, of the Vandals. **There are still two woes to come.** That is, two other serious persecutions.

13. **Then the sixth angel blew his trumpet,** This addresses the followers of the heretics among the Italians and the rulers in Constantinople.[7] To understand this, one must know that Emperor Anastasius, infected by the Eutychian heresy, began to rule in the year 493, and he reigned for twenty-five years. At the time, Theodoric, the Arian King, was ruling in Italy. At that time two popes were elected over against each other, Symmachus and Laurentius. This caused a great conflict among the Christians and among the clergy, leading to many murders. Finally, the Church rejected Laurentius and approved Symmachus. Moreover, Paschasius, the cardinal deacon, who was otherwise holy and faithful, erred in this, because he supported Laurentius to the best of his ability. As a result, after his death he was found in purgatory by Germanus, the Capuan Bishop, as St. Gregory relates in *The Dialogues*, Book 4.[8] These four men caused a great tribulation in the Church, namely, Laurentius and Symmachus over the papacy and Anastasius and Theodoric by their zeal for heresies. Seeing the Catholic clergy contending with one another to the point of murder, they

thought less of the Church than before and similarly catholic doctrine; as a result they were incited to persecute it. And these four are called angels here, because in this book the name *angel* is indifferently assigned to good and evil persons, as was clear above.

These things having been set out in advance, he proceeds because he considers first the tribulation of the Church and second its consolation in the following chapter. The first is in two parts, namely, a principal and an incidental part, which begins at the place: **The rest of humankind,** (9:20).

Concerning the first it is said: **Then the sixth angel blew his trumpet,** Namely, Laurentius, who, by a rebellious attempt and prideful word, aspired to the papacy. **And I heard a voice** Namely, the voice of Cardinal Paschasius from the college of the Church in Rome, who in the election gave his support to Laurentius and sustained his cause against the freedom of the Church.

14. **Saying to the sixth angel** That is, Laurentius. **"Release the four angels who are bound at the great river Euphrates."** That is, in the Roman Empire, which is called the great river because of the great number of peoples living there; therefore it says in chapter 17: **"The waters . . . are peoples and multitudes . . ."** (17:15). It is also called the Euphrates, because, just as the Euphrates is the fourth river of paradise (Gn 2:14), so also among the four principal kingdoms, the Roman Kingdom is called the fourth (Dn 2:40). In this Empire the four angels, namely, Laurentius, Symmachus, Anastasius, and Theodoric, were the legates who were held back before the election of Laurentius, inasmuch as they ceased from disturbing the Church. When he was elected, however,

they were incited to trouble the Church as has been said above, and therefore it is added:

15. **"So the four angels were released, who had been held ready for the hour,"** Namely, to throw the Church continuously into confusion. One should know that by supporting Laurentius, Paschasius did not intend this confusion, but because he was followed and despite his intention gave his voice to the election of Laurentius, therefore, it is said concerning Laurentius **So the four angels were released . . .** That through his ambition the other three proceeded to attack the Church. **To kill a third of humankind.** This third part indicates the catholic people, as was said above in chapter 4, which in great part was killed by the evil adherents of Laurentius and similarly by those adhering to Symmachus; partly by the heretical emperor, Anastasius, who sent many bishops into exile and afflicted many Catholics; partly by Theodoric, the Arian king, who wished to destroy all Italy insofar as they were orthodox. He martyred St. John, the pope, and Symmachus and Boethius—most distinguished men and consuls as it is reported in the *Legend of St. John Pope and Martyr.*[9]

16. **The number of the troops of the calvary** That is, followers of the four and of those causing them to disrupt Christians. **Was two hundred million;** This number is put here as a determinate number for an indeterminate one, just as in chapter 4, and designates that there was a great multitude.

17. **And this was how I saw the horses:** That is, those subject to the four and obedient to them in evil and especially to Anastasius and Theodoric. **The riders wore** The four previously mentioned angels teaching them.

Wore breastplates Just as among good persons righteousness is called their shield (Eph 6:14), "Put on the shield of righteousness," so the opposite is the case here, unrighteousness is called the shield of the evil. **The color of fire** The fiery lust for doing harm. **And of sapphire** That is, of a celestial color in which the appearance of zealous faith is indicated, because the heretics assert that they have the truth of the faith and incite persecution against those who are truly catholic. **And of sulfur;** On account of the foulness of the vices in them and proceeding outward into evil works. **The heads of the horses** That is, the leaders of the evil ones obeying them. **Were like lions' heads,** By which their cruelty is noted. **And fire came from their mouths.** Namely, of emulation in relation to Symmachus and Laurentius. **And Smoke** Of vanity in relation to Anastasius. **And Sulfur** Of stench in relation to the Arian, Theodoric.

18. **By these three plagues a third of humankind was killed,** That is, a great part of the Christians in the manner mentioned earlier.

19. **For the power of the horses is in their mouths** That is, in the four leaders, just as the first part of the head is the mouth. **And in their tails;** That is, by their attendants following them to evil. **Their tails are like serpents,** Because of their serpentine cunning, which was theirs to persecute the catholics. **Having heads;** In armies there are tribunes and centurions and such, who are captains of those subject to them. **And with them they inflict harm.** For they incite their subjects to persecute the true Christians.

20. **The rest of humankind,** This is the incidental part, because in this book John describes the status of the

Church at the time of King Theodoric, about whom he had just spoken. A great massacre occurred among the pagans who were not from the Church, and thus this is described incidentally.[10] At that time the Saxons fought against the Thuringians, and many of them were slain here and there, which was said earlier about the Christians in the persecution of Anastasius and Theodoric, and this is what is said: **The rest of humankind,** Namely, of the Saxons and of the Thuringians who do not confess Christ. **Who were not killed in these plagues,** That is, killed by a physical and eternal death for the faith in Christ; this is a manner of speech, which among the Hebrews is called "cut off," as in 2 Sm 5:8, "David had said on that day, "Whoever would strike down the Jebusites . . ." Nevertheless, this does not say how this battle would be, but it is added that he would be the leader of the army, as it is said in 1 Chr 11:6. Therefore with this in mind, these were not only dead physically but also eternally in hell, and the reason is provided when it is said: **They did not repent of their [works]**[11] That is, from their sins, and five kinds of sins are noted, namely, many idolatries, numerous murders and sorceries, fornication, and thefts. And the letter is plain.

Notes

1. Vincent of Beauvais, *The Mirror of History* (in 31 books) is a universal history of humankind from creation until 1254; it was one of the standard encyclopedic works of the late Middle Ages.

2. Emperor Valentinian I (364–75); for a discussion of this complicated period of history in the western Empire and this orthodox

emperor's relationship to Arianism, see W. H. C. Frend, *The Rise of Christianity* (Philadelphia: Fortress Press, 1984), pp. 617ff.

3. The Psalm verse continues, "They repented and sought God earnestly."

4. Gaiseric († 477), who as ruler of the Vandals, preceded his son Huneric (477–84) and one of Huneric's successors, Thrasamund (496–523), is listed last in Nicholas's order. He was the most important of the three. This citation was not found in Gregory's *Dialogue* 4.

5. A section is omitted because Nicholas becomes redundant.

6. The biblical text only notes two languages.

7. As promised, Nicholas will now turn to the followers of the heretics.

8. Nicholas has borrowed this whole discussion from Alexander and Peter, including the reference to Germanus's finding Paschasius in purgatory. See Alexander (pp. 145ff.) and Peter (pp. 485ff.). See also Gregory, *Dialogue* 4, 42.

9. See Peter, p. 484.

10. The historiography of these commentators properly applies only to Church history, and, therefore, this incident from world history is only an aside.

11. The word "works" is not in the text. This comment indicates how Lyra could range over the Bible to interpret a passage from the Apocalypse and to make a gruesome Old Testament passage morally acceptable.

Chapter 10

THE CONSOLATION OF THE CHURCH
UNDER JUSTIN I, JUSTINIAN, AND JUSTIN II

1. **And I saw** Having described the tribulation of the Church, here John describes its consolation, and first he presents the consolation; second the fruit of piety in the following chapter. The first is in two parts, because he includes first the consolation by the Emperor Justin; and second its continuation through his nephew, Justinian,[1] at the place: **Then the voice that I had heard** (10:8).

Concerning the first, one should know that the elder Justin ruled for ten years after the heretical Anastasius, beginning in the year 518. In his love for the Christian religion he fervently wanted to separate the Arian churches in the East and to consecrate Catholic bishops. However, he did not accomplish this, since he was hindered by the requests of Pope John to protect all the Christians in Italy from being killed by the Arian king, Theodoric, who, nevertheless, later killed St. John, as was said. Therefore, it is said here of Justin: **And I saw another mighty angel** The imperial power. **Coming down from heaven,** By baptismal regeneration in the Church militant. **Wrapped in a cloud,** Of baptismal grace. **With a rainbow over his head;** Because he proclaimed the peace of the Church. For the rainbow is the sign of a covenant (Gn 9:13). **His face was like the sun,** On account of the splendor of his face. **And his legs like pillars of fire.** By the feet the affections are understood, because just as the feet move the body, so the affections move the soul. Moreover, Justin's affections burned with the fire of love to promote Christianity.

2. He held a little scroll open in his hand. Because he wrote and sent letters throughout the empire to favor the Christians. **Setting his right foot on the sea and his left foot on the land,** He wrote to the inhabitants on the land and on the islands of the sea. Or otherwise, by "the sea," because it contains water, the Christian people is understood regenerated by the water of baptism. The land, because the pagans are fixed on earthly desires; there were many of each in the empire of Justin, but he was more favorable to the Christians, on account of which it is said: **He set his right foot on the sea.**

3. **He gave a great shout** Giving orders by his imperial authority. **Like a lion roaring.** To the terror of the Arians, whence it is said in Prv 20, "The dread anger of a king is like the growling of a lion." Just as this shout was a terror to the Arians, so it was a consolation to the Christians, therefore it is added: **And when he shouted, the seven thunders sounded.** All the churches are designated by the number seven, because the whole is designated by seven, as it is said in St. Gregory, *Homily* 25.[2] He shouted in a voice to the praise of God. Nevertheless, Justin did not complete what he intended against the Arians, because of what was said earlier.

4. John was prohibited from writing it, whence it is said: **"Seal up what the seven thunders have said. . . ."**

5. **Then the angel** Here the consolation of the Church is described, promised through the angel of Justin. One should know that emperors and kings have two guardian angels, one as an individual person, just as the rest of humanity (Mt 18:10); "'Take care that you do not despise one of these little ones; for, I tell you, in heaven their angels continually see the face of my Father in heaven'."

(These angels are from a lower rank); the other by reason of the dignity or of the office. For there are angels in command of each kingdom which are called commanders, and they are from a superior rank of the lower hierarchy. These are the guardians, especially, of kings, insofar as the kingdoms virtually depend on them. Therefore, they are called princes in the Scripture (Dn 10:21, "There is no one with me who contends against these princes except Michael, your prince"). And in the same place, "When I am through with him, the prince of Greece will come" (Dn 10:20). Thus these angels are finally understood for the kings or the kingdoms whom they command, and thus it is in the design, as will be seen in what proceeds. Therefore, he says, **Then the angel whom I saw** That is, the angel of Justin by reason of his rule.[3]

Raised his right hand and swore To declare the future event. **"There will be no more delay."** This does not mean the simple cessation of time, because after the blowing of the trumpet of the seventh angel in this book a large course of history is described up to the end of the world.[4] It refers to the cessation of the success of the Arian heresy, as will be seen in the following chapter, because this was fulfilled at the time of the younger Justin, who was the third emperor from this elder Justin.[5] On account of which it is clear that what is said here concerning the angel standing on the sea and on the land, which raised his hand and swore, cannot mean the elder Justin, because he did not know about things that must happen after his death, but his angel knew by divine revelation. The elder Justin's desire to destroy the Arian heresy (which was impeded as was discussed above) would be completed at the time of the younger Justin, which the angel foreknew, and thus swore.

7. **"When the seventh angel is to blow his trumpet,"** In the beginning of the rule of the younger Justin this was completed, as will be seen. **"The mystery of God will be fulfilled,"** That is, the secret. **"As he announced to his servants the prophets."** Who foretold that the Lord Jesus Christ would reign with his faithful, and thus at the time of the seventh angel the Christians prevailed against the unfaithful heretics. Thus John heard voices from heaven, **"The kingdom of the world has become the kingdom of our Lord and of his Messiah,"** as it is said in the following chapter (11:15).

8. **Then the voice that I had heard from heaven** Here the continuation of the consolation of the Church by Emperor Justinian is included, who in the beginning of his reign was truly catholic. He began to rule in the year 528. He was a literate man, abbreviated the Roman laws, and compiled them in one volume called *Justinian's Digest* in which he put many laws favorable to the Christians, concerning which John says here: **Then the voice that I had heard** That was the voice of the angel through whom Christ was speaking to John, as has been said in the first chapter of this book. **"Go, and take the scroll"** That is, *Justinian's Digest*, which John must receive, because it was favorable to the Church, as has been said. **"That is open in the hand"** This was the angel for Justinian's rule, as will be seen.

9. **And he said to me, "Take it, and eat;"** Like a most delectable thing in the mouth. **"It will be bitter"** Because at the end of his life Justinian was corrupted by heresy, and his remembrance contained in the book became bitter to the faithful, which in the beginning of his

life was sweet. Thus it is clear how this angel who handed the book to John was not Justinian; for he did not foresee his fall into heresy, but his angel speaking to John added:

11. **"You must prophesy again about many peoples and nations and languages and kings."** Because afterwards, John wrote prophetically in this book concerning many nations and peoples.

Notes

1. Justin (518–27) and Justinian, his nephew (527–65).

2. Gregory, Sermon 33 in *The Sermons on the Gospels*, in reference to Lk 7:36–50 (*PL* 76:1239C).

3. Here an infrequent principle applies, namely, that an angel can represent the guardian angel of a ruler.

4. In this linear method of interpreting the Apocalypse the amount of book left in the Apocalypse affected how a particular passage could be interpreted, because the whole course of history had to be included.

5. Justin II, who ruled from 565–78.

Chapter 11
THE TWO WITNESSES: SILVERIUS AND MENAS; ENOCH AND ELIJAH; THE DOUBLE LITERAL SENSE

1. **Then I was given a measuring rod like a staff,** After the consolation of the Church he addresses the fruit of devotion, and, second, John returns to the burden of a

certain tribulation for the Church at the place, **"And they will trample over the holy city . . ."** (11:2). Concerning the first, one must know that Pope Felix, who presided over the Roman Church at the time, instituted a feast of dedication of the church to be celebrated every year. For the dedication the bishop encircles the church and conducts himself as if he were measuring the eternal walls, and on the floor of the church from corner to corner he writes crosswise the Greek alphabet; thus, in a certain way, the interior is measured. According to this, John prophesies speaking in an image of the Church. **Then I was given a measuring rod** To dedicate the temple he carries an aspersory in his hand. **"Come and measure the temple"** This is the word of Pope Felix to every bishop to dedicate the church.

2. **"But do not measure the court outside the temple,"** This establishes that the mass is only to be celebrated in a consecrated place. **"For it is given over to the nations,"** Who offer their sacrifices not only in consecrated places but also in profane ones. **"And they will trample"** Here St. John returns to describing a certain tribulation of the Church incited by Anthimus, patriarch of Constantinople, who, because he had been corrupted by the Eutychian heresy was deposed by Pope Agapetus.[1] In his place the monk and servant of God, Menas, was instituted.[2] Nevertheless, Empress Theodora, infected by the same heresy, sought to restore Anthimus through Pope Silverius, as is clear in the *Legends of St. Silverius*.[3] Angered by his refusal to do this, Theodora and her husband Justinian, corrupted by the Eutychian heresy by Anthimus, began to persecute the ministers of the Church; thus Silverius was deposed and sent into exile by

Belisarius, the patrician, and Menas, the servant of God, was tormented in prison. And this is what John says **"Over the holy city"** That is, the Church, which is called the holy city, for it is the unity of the citizens gathered by the Holy Spirit. **"They will trample"** That is, Anthimus, Justinian, Theodora, and Belisarius by grievously oppressing the ministers of the Church. **"For forty-two months."** For such a period or thereabouts this persecution is said to have lasted, namely, for 3½ years.

3. **"And I will grant my two witnesses"** Supply perseverance and wisdom. These were Silverius and Menas, the servant of God, who stood steadfastly against the followers of the Eutychian heresy, by preaching the truth. Therefore it is added: **"Authority to prophesy for one thousand two hundred sixty days,"** These days equal the same as before, namely, 3½ years or thereabouts. **"Wearing sackcloth."** That is, with common vestments, because Pope Silverius was stripped of his papal garb and was dressed in monastic garb.

4. **These are the two olive trees** Because of the richness of their devotion. **And the two lampstands** Because of the ardor of their love. **That stand before the Lord of the earth.** By the steadfastness of the truth.

5. **And if anyone wants to harm them,** As was done by the noted persecutors of the Church. **Fire pours from their mouth** The words proceeding from the fervor of faith. **And consumes their foes;** By conferring on them the sentence of excommunication; therefore, it is added: **Anyone who wants to harm them** With the material sword. **Must be killed in this manner** With the spiritual sword.

6. **They have the authority to shut the sky** With the keys of the Church. **So that no rain may fall during the**

days of their prophesying, For the benefits of the Church are not offered to those justly excommunicated. **And they have authority over the waters** That is, the doctrines of the heretics, concerning whom it is said in Prv 9:17, "Stolen water is sweet." **To turn them into blood** By demonstrating their error. **And to strike the earth** The heretics fixed on earthly things, whence Augustine says, "If you love the earth, you are earth."[4] **With every kind of plague** To burden with the spiritual sentence of excommunication.

7. **When they have finished their testimony,** By constantly defending the truth. **The beast that comes up from the bottomless pit** That is, Belisarius, the patrician —to the extent that he was a cruel man, he is called a lion or a rabid dog. **Will make war on them** In the manner said before. **And kill them,** By civil death by sending them into exile.

8. **And their dead bodies will lie** They were considered common, just as a cadaver lying on the ground. **In the street of the great city** That is, among the congregation of the faithful, which at that point was very large. **Which is spiritually called Sodom** On account of the baseness of the vices. **And Egypt,** As a result of the obscurity of their errors, **Where also their Lord** Namely, Christ. **Was crucified.** Because he was preaching against the vices of the Scribes and Pharisees, they conceived invidious and hateful things against him, by which their understanding was obscured concerning Christ, which they had through the writing of the prophets, as I have said more fully concerning Mt 21:38, "The servants said to themselves, 'This is the heir'." Thus blinded they proceeded to kill him.

9. **Members of the peoples and tribes and languages and nations will gaze** Their civil death and exile to different peoples of diverse languages was noted. **For three and a half days** Here a day is understood as a year according to Ez 4:6, "I assign you, one day for each year." Their exile lasted that long, as was said before. **And refuse to let their dead bodies be placed in a tomb;** That is, the leaders of Eutychians by not letting them experience any human kindness.

10. **And the inhabitants of the earth** That is, the Eutychian heresy, which was dominant on earth. **Will gloat over them** Concerning their exile. **And exchange presents,** As a sign of joy. **Because these two prophets had been a torment** By excommunications and aggravations.

11. **But after three and a half days** That is, after 3½ years. **The breath of life from God entered them,** Because they were restored to their former state and were thus revivified from civil death. Silverius assumed the papal seat again in the year 536.[5] **And those who saw them were terrified.** That is, the Eutychians.

12. **Then they heard a great voice from heaven** That is, from the Church militant restoring them to their former honor. Nevertheless, St. Silverius after being returned to exile died there, and thus went to heaven with the martyr's crown; the same should be held concerning Menas, the servant of God; thus it is possible to expound this passage otherwise, **And I heard a great voice:** Namely, of the voice of God calling them to glory.

While their enemies watched them. Through their miracles witnessing to his glory. It is written in the *Legend of St. Silverius* that after his death in the place of exile, many came who were ill and were healed.

However, this passage discussed above is commonly interpreted to refer to Enoch and Elijah, who are said to be the future witnesses of Christ preaching against the wickedness of Antichrist for 3½ years. **"Wearing sackcloth."** (11:3) That is, in worthless clothing; they are called **two olive trees** because of their exuberant devotion, and **The two lampstands** (11:4) By the ardor of their love. **Standing** In the sight of God by their constancy against the wickedness of Antichrist. For here it is said that **Fire pours from their mouth** (11:5). That is, the word of fervent preaching by which the malice of Antichrist and of his own is disclosed, and the word of devoted prayer by which Antichrist and a great part of his army will be deservedly thunderstruck, just as it was more fully said in 2 Thes 2. Thus they perform true wonders over against the lying signs of Antichrist, by which Antichrist and his followers will be struck down. Therefore it is added: **They have authority** (11:6).

Finally, Antichrist, who is here called the beast because of his cruelty. **Rising from the bottomless pit** (11:7) Because of the power of his own demon. **Will kill them, and their dead bodies will lie in the street** (11:8) To terrorize the Christians. **Of the great city** That is, of the congregation adhering to Antichrist, which will be especially great. **Called Sodom and Egypt,** That is, vile and shadowy. **Members of the peoples and tribes and languages and nations will gaze** (11:9) Because from all the nations many will follow Antichrist. **For three and a half days** Namely, natural days and a part of a fourth. **And the inhabitants of the earth will gloat** (11:10) That is, the followers of Antichrist. **But after three and a half**

days, the breath of life. . . . (11:11) Because they will be resuscitated and transferred to heaven as a testimony to the truth of their preaching.

This exposition harmonizes with the text more than the preceding one. Both, nevertheless, are able to be called literal.[6] It should be known that a figure of another thing is necessarily something in itself, because what is nothing cannot figure or signify something. Therefore a figure can be taken in three ways. In one way only as the thing in and of itself. In another way only as the figure of another. In the third way as the thing in itself and the figure of another. This threefold manner is frequently found in the Holy Scriptures by the gift of the word.

Concerning Solomon it is said in I Kgs 11:4, "His wives turned away his heart after other gods." This is said only with reference to himself and in no way as the figure of Christ that he was, and thus the literal sense (*sensus literalis*) refers only to Solomon. This is what is said concerning him [Solomon] in Ps 72:17, "Blessed be his name forever, enduring as long as the sun." This is not to be understood as referring to Solomon in and of himself, but only as he was a figure of Christ—on account of which the literal sense refers only to Christ; just as in the same place it was proclaimed more fully. That, moreover, which the Lord said concerning him in 2 Sm 7:14, "I will be a father to him, and He shall be a son to me" is understood to refer to Solomon himself and that he was a figure of Christ, because he was the son of God through the grace of adoption, especially in the beginning of his reign, as is clear in 2 Sm. He was a figure of Christ, who is the son of God by nature, which sonship is more perfect than the other.

Thus there is a double literal sense (*duplex sensus literalis*); one referring to Solomon by reason of his adoptive sonship; the other referring to Christ by reason of his natural sonship figured through this. In this second way the Apostle intends the noted passage in Heb 1:5 to prove the divinity of Christ, which proof is not effectively done through Scripture, unless it is understood in the literal sense, as Augustine says against Vincent the Donatist.[7]

Thus the double literal sense is in the case in question. One was fulfilled in Pope Silverius and Menas, servant of God, who were figures of Enoch and Elijah; the other will be fulfilled in Enoch and Elijah, with whom the letter agrees more, as was seen, and will be fulfilled more perfectly in them; therefore the sense principally intended refers to them.[8]

13. **At that moment there was a great earthquake,** After the description of the persecution of the Church by the Vandals and the leaders of Constantinople and the Italians, here the persecution by the Goths, who were Arians, is included, as it has been said above in chapter 8. It is divided in three parts: In the first, the persecution of the Goths is placed; in the second, their destruction, at the place: **Then the seventh angel** (11:15); and in the third, the increase of devotion, at the place: **Then God's temple was opened,** (11:19). Concerning the first, it should be known that at the time that Justinian and Theodora and Anthimus were persecuting the ministers of the Church, Pope Vigilius having been sent with a rope around his neck was dragged through Constantinople, and the clergy who had been led away with him were condemned to work the mines in diverse places.[9] Therefore, Totila, King

of the Goths, having gathered a great army, invaded the Empire and, wandering over many provinces, devastated Italy.[10] He killed St. Herculanus, Bishop of Perugia, with the people of the city and many other Christians in various provinces.[11] This is what is said, **At that moment** That is, at the time Justinian was corrupted by the Arian heresy—soon after the death of Silverius and Menas, servant of God, who were just mentioned. **There was a great earthquake,** That is, a great disturbance for those living in the land as a result of the king, Totila, as has been said. **And a tenth of the city fell;** That is, a great part of the Christian people—the tenth part or as close as one can estimate. **Seven thousand people were killed in the earthquake,** That is, people by name. **Seven thousand** That is, a great number. Here a determinate number is used for an indeterminate one, as in chapter 4 above. **And the rest were terrified** That is, the Roman people feared greatly when Totila took hold of the city; nevertheless, because he neither killed the people nor burned the city, it is added: **And gave glory to the God of heaven.** To God for their escape.

14. **The second woe has passed.** That is, this tribulation. **The third woe is coming very soon.** Namely, the destruction of the Goths, and therefore this woe was not on the catholics. Likewise it was said in chapter 8, **"Woe, woe to the inhabitants of the earth"** That is, catholics and the Arians combined.

15. **Then the seventh angel** Here the destruction of the Goths is described. Justin the younger succeeded Justinian as Emperor and began to reign in the year 566.[12] Moreover, he appointed Narses, a patrician of the Romans and a man strenuous in arms, and sent him to suppress the

Goths. Having gathered a great army he conquered the Goths and killed their king; thus Italy was liberated from them, and served Christ in fear. And this is what is said, **And the Seventh angel** That is, Emperor Justin. **Blew his trumpet,** He sent Narses into Italy by imperial authority. **And there were loud voices in heaven,** That is, in the Church militant, because after the Goths were killed the Church broke out in shouts of divine praise. **Saying, "The kingdom of the world. . . ."** Freed from the Goths and the rest of Arians, Italy, where Rome is and the head of the Kingdom of Christ on earth, served Christ freely.

16. **Then the twenty-four elders** That is, all of the bishops and their churches, as was said in chapter 4. **"We give you thanks,"** Concerning the liberation of the Church to whom the news of the event arrived.

18. **"The nations raged,"** That is, the Goths because of the killing of their king and their destruction. **"But your wrath has come,"** That is, your punishment of the Goths, because when God punishes, God is angry in a certain manner of speaking, as was frequently discussed above. **"And the time for judging the dead,"** That is, the punishment of the Goths in behalf of the Catholics, who were killed by them. **"For rewarding your servants,"** Because among those killed by the Goths there were some great preachers who are called "prophets" announcing future punishments and rewards, some saints, and some "great" in the world, and others who were small and in between. **"And for destroying those"** That is, the Goths and the other Arians. **"Who destroy the earth."** Corporeally by words of false doctrine.[13]

19. **Then God's temple in heaven was opened,** Here, thirdly, the increase of devotion is included. At that

time a great plague affected Constantinople, for which the feast of the purification of the Blessed Mary was instituted to be solemnly celebrated on February 2, when the Blessed Virgin presented her son in the temple, which is called the "ark of the covenant." In that place the fullness of knowledge and of truth was designated by the tablets and of power by the vessel and of devotion by the manna—all three of which were in the ark. The plague ceased, and this is what is said, **Then God's temple in heaven was opened,** That is, the Church militant in which the material temple was opened to solemnly celebrate the feast. **And the ark of the covenant was seen** That is, Christ, whose offering and presentation in the temple through St. Simeon and Anna the prophetess was memorialized in the Feast of Purification, which spread from Constantinople to other parts of the world. Therefore, it is added: **There were flashes** That is, burning torches like "flashes." **And peals** Of divine praise. **Of thunder,** Of holy preaching. **An earthquake,** Many of the earthly people were moved to devotion. **And heavy hail.** Because the power of the demon causing this pestilence was repressed.

Notes

1. Anthimus, bishop of Trebizond, succeeded Epiphanius as patriarch of Constantinople. Although a delegate to Chalcedon he became a Monophysite sympathizer. Pope Agapetus (535–36) asked him to step down because of canon 15 of the Council of Nicea, which forbade bishops to be transferred from one see to another. See Alexander, pp. 229, 230.

2. The Alexandrian-born Menas (March 13, 536).

3. Pope Silverius (536–37). Nicholas has taken this account from Peter; see pp. 491–92. It is important to note that, in the middle of this account in chapter 11, Peter remarks that all these different historical issues and figures in history show that John was interested in much more than the coming of the Antichrist. De-emphasizing the role of the antichrist was crucial to the agendas of these moderate Franciscans, Peter and Nicholas, in contrast to the more radical commentaries in the Olivian tradition (see the introduction).

4. There is a similar passage in Augustine's *In Epistolam Johannis ad Parthos*, Tractate 2, Chapter 2 (*PL* 35:1997). "Do you love the earth? To earth you shall turn." See *Ten Homilies on the First Epistle of St. John* in *Augustine: Later Works*, ed. John Burnaby, The Library of Christian Classics (Philadelphia: Westminster Press, 1955), p. 278.

5. Silverius was pope from 536 to 537.

6. The following excursus in the text is one of the few descriptions of Nicholas's famous double-literal sense. The *locus classicus* is 2 Sm 7:14–15 and its biblical commentary in Heb 1:5. The biblical parallels for this passage are 1 Chr 22:7–10 and 17:13, 14. See "Nicholas of Lyra, Apocalypse Commentator, Historian and Critic," pp. 59–61.

7. Alluding to St. Augustine's famous letter (Ep. 93.8, 24) to Donatus, who was really a Rogatist, the issue of theological arguments needing to be based on the literal and not on the spiritual senses was common. Thomas Aquinas makes this clear in *The Summa Theologiae* I^a, Q. 1, a.10.

8. The interesting thing to note about Nicholas's use of the double-literal sense in chapter 11 is that both literal meanings are in the future for John, neither pair (Silverius and Menas; Enoch and Elijah) is contemporary with him, and yet he thinks that Enoch and Elijah more literally fulfill the context of the passage.

---

9. Pope from 537. This would have been during the Three Chapters Controversy. He was arrested at Mass on November 22, 545, by the Byzantine police in Rome and brought to Constantinople via Sicily (*Oxford Dictionary of the Popes*, J. N. D. Kelly [Oxford and New York: Oxford University Press, 1986]).

10. Totila, the Ostrogoth, began to rally the Goths in Italy to beseige Rome at the end of 545.

11. See Alexander, p. 245, and Gregory, *Dial.* III, 11.

12. Justin II (565–78); Narses ended the Gothic resistance. See John Bagnell Bury, *A History of the Later Roman Empire. From Arcadius to Irene (395 A.D. to 800 A.D.)*, 2 vols. (New York: Dover, 1958), 2: 263ff.

13. The Basel 1498 edition of Lyra's *Literal Postill* differs on this verse making a distinction, which is probably the correct text, between a corporeal killing with weapons and a spiritual killing with words of false doctrine.

Chapter 12
THE PAGANS, SARACENS, SCHISMATICS, AND DISCIPLES OF ANTICHRIST

1. **A great portent** After describing the attack on the Church by the heretics noted above, here he describes the attack on them by heretics more broadly defined: the pagans, Saracens, schismatics, the disciples of Antichrist, and other heretics, as they are able to be called. According to this, the main parts will appear in what follows in this book. First, the attack by the pagans is discussed: first, under Chosroes, King of the Persians; second, under his successor in the following chapter. The first is in two

parts, because first the condition of the Church is described; second the persecution of Chosroes, at the place: **Then another portent appeared:** (12:3).

First, it should be known that when Phocas was Emperor, who began to rule in A.D. 605, the Persians under King Chosroes, who were waging a most grievous war, invaded many Roman provinces and Jerusalem itself. They destroyed the holy churches, profaning the sacred places, and, among the sacred ornaments which they took, they carried away the standard of the Lord's cross, as it is reported in the *Legend of the Exaltation of the Holy Cross.*[1] Therefore, the afflicted Christian Church was tortured until it brought forth a Christian son, who would liberate it from the affliction of Chosroes and his followers, and this is what is said: **A great portent** Of the Church militant.

A woman That is, the Church generally, and specifically the one in Jerusalem, which was joined with Christ as a woman with a man. **Clothed with the sun,** That is, with Christ, who is the sun of Justice (Gal 3:27), "As many of you as were baptized into Christ have clothed yourselves with Christ." For he himself is the husband and bridegroom of the Church. **With the moon under her feet,** That is, all that is mutable and defective signified by the moon, whose condition ought to pertain to the lowest parts of the Church (1 Cor 6:4), "If you have ordinary cases, then, do you appoint as judges those who have no standing in the church?" **And on her head a crown** That is, the preaching of the twelve apostles, which shone brightly in the primitive Church, which is called its "head" in a manner of speaking; any beginning of anything is commonly called its head.

2. **She was pregnant** In anguish she called to God, so that God would quickly give to her a son who would free her from the oppression of the infidels.

3. **Then another portent appeared** Here the persecution of Chosroes is described and, second, the liberation of the Church, at the place: **And she gave birth to a son.** (12:5) Concerning the first he says: **Then another portent** That is, Chosroes, king of the Persians, who was seen in heaven (the Church militant) as a serious persecutor of the Church, and it is added: **A great ruddy dragon** Because of his cunning and deceit. **A great** Because of the magnitude of his power. **Ruddy** That is, "red" because of the pouring of much blood. That "ruddy" is understood in a certain manner for "red" is clear in 1 Sm 16:12, where it is said concerning David: "That he was ruddy . . . and was handsome." That is, "ruddy" according to the commentators.[2] It is said also of Chosroes because he burned the churches and the sacred places. **With seven heads** That is, the six kings subject to him, and he himself was the seventh, whence it is added: **And seven diadems on his heads.** Because they are the royal signs. **And ten horns** That is, the ten battle lines in his army, whence in 1 Mc the battle line set to fight is called a horn where it is said, "Bacchides was on the right wing . . ." (1 Mc 9:12).

Others explain it a different way, in that by the seven heads all the leaders subject to him are understood and by the seven horns all of his warriors. "Seven" is understood as "all" sometimes, because all time is comprehended by replication in seven days, and similarly the number ten because the numbers following are replications of ten or its parts, as it is said in Book 3 of the *Physics.*

4. **And his tail** That is, the army following him, **Swept down a third of the stars** Of the faithful who are called stars in the Scripture: "Today you are as numerous as the stars of heaven" (Dt 1:10). For with his army Chosroes killed many Christians in Egypt and Libya and the Holy Land and other places, and he led others into captivity; it was estimated to include a third part of the Christians living in these lands. Similarly in a manner of speaking, Dn 8:10 speaks of Antiochus Epiphanes, "That it [a horn] threw down to the earth some of the host of the stars, and trampled on them." **Then the dragon stood** Because Chosroes lay in wait in every way to kill any Christian leader who rose to defend the Church. Here the liberation of the Church is described, and it is divided in two parts, because first he makes the main point; second, he declares a certain assurance, at the place: **The woman was given the two wings of the great eagle** (12:14). The first is again in three parts: first, the birth of Emperor Heraclius is included; second, the conquering of Chosroes, at the place: **And war broke out** (12:7); and third, the oppression of those subdued, at the place: **"Woe to the earth and the sea,"** (12:12).

5. Concerning the first it is said: **And she gave birth to a son,** Namely, the Catholic Heraclius, who, after the death of Phocas, ruled for thirty years and began to rule in the year 613.[3] **A male child,** This is added to denote that he was a vigorous man and experienced in arms, as is said in the *Legend of the Exaltation of the Holy Cross.* **Who is to rule all the nations** Because he ruled the Roman Empire—those who rebelled he vanquished by the sword. **But her child was snatched away** That is, placed in the protection of God. God protected Heraclius against the

machinations and the deceit of Chosroes by which he sought to kill him.

6. **And the woman fled** For the Church of Asia fearful of Chosroes crossed the sea, which is called the Strait of St. George, and fled into Greece, which is here called solitude, not because it was not inhabited, but is called a fugitive solitude, in a manner of speaking by which fugitives in another land are said to be there as if in exile or in a desert. **So that there she can be nourished** The Christians living there. **For one thousand two hundred sixty days** Which make three and a half years, and within this same chapter this woman is spoken about: **Where she is nourished for a time, and times, and a half a time** (12:14). That is, for three years and a half; for "a time" in the singular in sacred Scripture signifies one year, and the plural without the number signifies two years, as was said more fully in Dn 12. These times added to the seven years equal the duration of the war between the Persians and Heraclius.

7. **And a great war broke out** This describes the destruction of Chosroes; second, on account of this the thanksgiving, at the place: **Then I heard a loud voice** (12:10).

Concerning the first it is said: **And a great war broke out** Between the Persians and Heraclius. **Great** Namely, intense, since there were many soldiers on both sides and extensive, because it lasted a long time as it was said. **Michael and his angels** Some expound this as the archangel, Michael, who is the prince of the Church, just as in the Old Testament he was the leader of the synagogue (Dn 10). Therefore, he stood with his angels to protect and direct Heraclius and his army who fought for the Church.

But because the dragon and his angels are understood to be Chosroes and his army by all expositors, similarly, it is more convenient that Michael and his angels be understood to be Heraclius and his soldiers. "Michael" means "One like God." Heraclius in this war was the vicar of God for the Church. And from what has been said before, it is clear that in this book good and evil persons are frequently called angels.

8. **They were defeated,** Namely, Chosroes and his men, but more often they were vanquished. **And there was no longer any place for them in heaven.** That is, in the Church, because Heraclius pursuing Chosroes drove him from Ethiopia and Libya and the Holy Land, where the Church was thriving earlier, and compelled him to return disgracefully to his own land; therefore it is added:

9. **The great dragon was thrown down,** Nevertheless, because Chosroes himself was in his old age, he quickly handed over the kingdom to his son, as will be said later. **Who is called the Devil,** For his excessive evil, just as a wicked person is commonly called a devil or Satan. **The deceiver of the whole world.** He made his subjects worship him as God. Therefore, it is said in the *Legend of the Exaltation of the Holy Cross* that he had made a silver tower in which he constructed a golden throne with transparent gems. There he had set up a fourfold image of the sun, the moon, and the stars, and he had arranged hidden pipes and channels such that rain poured from above, as if he were God. This is why it is said: **The whole world.** But it should not be understood that he himself subjected the whole world to himself, but it is a hyperbole to designate that he subjected a great part of the world to himself; in this way, he deceived, just as

it is commonly said, "The whole city went to the show," although most stayed home. **He was thrown down** Because with his army he was forced to take refuge in his own land.

10. **Then I heard a loud voice** Here the thanksgiving of the Church's children is included because of the destruction of Chosroes. **In heaven,** That is, of the Church militant. **"Now have come the salvation"** Because freed from the oppression of Chosroes, the faithful could serve Christ. **"For the accuser of our comrades has been thrown down,"** That is, of the Christians whom he made accusable before God by impelling them to do evil things and forcing them to worship him, as it has been said.

11. **"But they have conquered him by the blood of the Lamb"** This does not refer to these same Christians, but to those who did not acquiesce to him, choosing rather to die, and thus they were victors through the martyr's crown. Therefore, it is added: **"They did not cling to life"** That is, the corporeal life, as it is recorded in Ps 78:34, "When he killed them, they sought for him." One should understand here not those who were killed but others of the same people.

12. **"Rejoice then, you heavens"** For the glorification of the martyrs and the destruction of Chosroes. **"But woe to the earth"** Here he describes the oppression of those subject to Chosroes, who was forced to return to his own land fiercely angry, and he began to burden his subjects by many exactions and extortions in order to multiply his soldiers to defend his kingdom from Emperor Heraclius. This is what is said: **"Woe to the earth and the sea,"** Because he was ruling not only in the desert but also in the many islands of the sea and because goods

were transported by sea he increased the fees and tolls. **"For the devil has come down to you"** That is, Chosroes having fled, who was called the Devil in the preceding part, as has been seen. **"Because he knows that his time is short!"** He was already an old man, and thus he did not have the time left to be able to conquer Heraclius; therefore he handed the kingdom over to his son.

13. **So when the dragon saw** Although he had persecuted the Church, especially outside his own land, now he began to increase its troubles in his own land where many Christians subject to his tribute lived. He began to persecute them more severely, not only through their possessions but also physically, just as Sennacherib, fleeing from Hezekiah, king of Judah, as a result of the defeat of his army, began to grievously afflict the Jews living in his own land (Tb 1:18).

14. **But the woman was given two wings** Here he declares what was said earlier, namely, how the woman clothed with the sun fled into solitude; this was with the help of Heraclius. Therefore, it is said: **The woman was given** The eagle is the symbol of the Roman Empire, therefore Heraclius is understood. His wings are the battle lines of his army, and by one wing the military battle line is signified, but they are called two here to preserve the metaphor, because a bird does not fly with one wing but with two. Moreover it is said that the armies of Heraclius helped the Christian Church to abide under the king of the Persians, because Heraclius sent soldiers from Greece to receive fleeing Christians from Persia; or because he was invading the edges of the kingdom of the Persians so forcefully that Chosroes's soldiers were totally occupied and the Christians could the more easily cross into

Greece. Or in either way. **Where she is nourished for a time,** That is, for 3½ years, as was said above.

15. **Then from his mouth the serpent poured water like a river** That is, many people, according to what is said in chapter 17:15, **"The waters . . . are peoples and multitudes,"** to kill the fleeing Christians.

16. **But the earth came to the help of the woman;** That is, the inhabitants of Greece or the soldiers of Heraclius in the way mentioned earlier. **And swallowed** Because the people sent by Chosroes were destroyed.

17. **Then the dragon was angry** That is, with the catholic people. **And went off to make war** That is, with the Christians, who were not able to flee with the others or with Heraclius and his army lest they invade the kingdom of the Persians.

18. **Then the dragon took his stand** The sea, which is a gathering of waters is understood to be the kingdom of Chosroes, which was especially populous. The seashore on the edge of the sea is understood to mean the edges of the Persian kingdom, in which the army of Chosroes stood to prevent Heraclius and his army from crossing.

Notes

1. See Alexander, pp. 260–61.

2. This is one of Nicholas's many uses of intertextuality; he ranges over the whole Bible interpreting Scripture with Scripture.

3. Actually Heraclius began to rule in 610–11.

Chapter 13
THE CHURCH UNDER CHOSROES II;
THE WAR BETWEEN THE PERSIANS AND HERACLIUS;
MUHAMMAD: THE SECOND BEAST

1. **And I saw** Having described the persecution of the Church under Chosroes, here the same is described under his son who succeeded him, and it is divided in three parts. First, the succession of the realm is described; second, the course of the battle, at the place: **And I saw** (13:3); and third, the end of the war of the Persians and Heraclius, at the place: **Let anyone who has an ear** (13:9).

Concerning the first John says: **And I saw a beast rising from the sea**, That is, from the Kingdom of the Persians, as has been said before. **A beast** That is, the son of Chosroes, who was living like a beast. **Rising** Through the power of the Kingdom of Persia, **Having** It is explained as in the preceding chapter concerning his father. **And on its horns were ten diadems,** This he says, because he paid his captains nearly the reward of kings so that they would fight more valiantly against Heraclius. **And on its heads were blasphemous names.** Because the captains blasphemed Christ, just as their princes did, as will be shown in the following part.

2. **And the beast that I saw was like a leopard,** Because of the variety of vices in which he had obstinately pursued, according to what Jeremiah says in chapter 13:23, "Can Ethiopians change their skin or leopards their spots? Then also you can do good who are accustomed to do evil." **Its feet were like a bear's,** Having huge feet to trample; thus he was panting to oppress the Church. **And**

its mouth was like a lion's mouth. On account of his cruelty. **And the dragon gave it his power** Because his father Chosroes handed the kingdom over to him sitting in his silver tower, as is said in the *Legend of the Exaltation of the Holy Cross*. **And great authority.** That is, a strong army to fight against Heraclius.

Here the progress of the battle is described; some expositors say here that the army of Heraclius and that of the son of Chosroes met near the Danube, and, through mutual agreement, Heraclius and the son of Chosroes fought each other one on one by a pact. The agreement was that the vanquished with his whole people would be subject to the victor.[1] Moreover, Heraclius stood out as the victor, and thus the son of Chosroes with his whole people submitted themselves to him.

3. According to this John says: **And I saw that one of its heads** That is, the first and principle head; for in the sacred Scripture "one" is sometimes used for "first," as in Gn 1:5, "And there was evening and there was morning, 'one' day"; that is, "first." Thus this "one" head was the son of Chosroes, who was one of the seven heads of the beast, just as was said in the preceding chapter concerning Chosroes, his father. **Seemed to have received a death-blow,** That is, conquered and subjected to Heraclius, because by this he was not simply killed; therefore, it does not say killed absolutely, but **Seemed to have received a death-blow, but its mortal wound had been healed.** Because afterwards he rebelled against Heraclius, and thus he was cured from his subjection. This is what follows:

4. **They worshipped the beast, saying, "Who is like the beast?"** That is, no one. This does not concur with the earlier exposition, because that he rebelled after having

been defeated by Heraclius is not an argument that he was invincible, but much more the opposite. He had already been defeated by Heraclius, and his father was defeated more decidedly. Moreover, these expositors say that this rebellion was after the withdrawal of Heraclius from Persia, since Chosroes had been killed and the wood of the cross of the Lord was carried back; this, however, is said: **In amazement the whole world followed the beast,** (13:3) On account of his healing.

They worshipped the dragon, Through whom Chosroes is understood. Nevertheless, they worshipped him not after his death but before, as has been said above. Because of this, there is another way of explaining the passage about the deadly wound of the son of Chosroes. In one conflict, wounded against all human hope, he was healed quickly, and the people subject to him believed that he had a divine power in him that had healed him—just as they had worshipped his father, as has been said. According to which it is said: **One of its heads** That is, the son of Chosroes, by reason of what has been said. **Seemed to have received a death-blow,** That is, mortally wounded. **But its mortal wound had been healed.** Unexpectedly. **In amazement** On account of such a cure.

And they worshipped the dragon, That is, Chosroes, who gave his power to the beast, by handing the realm to his son. **And they worshipped the beast,** That is, the son of Chosroes, believing that there was something divine in him. **Saying, "Who is like the beast?"** That is, no one—because if he was wounded in battle he would be healed again.

5. **The beast was given a mouth uttering haughty and blasphemous words,** Through ostentation and

blasphemies against Christ and the Church. **And it was allowed to exercise authority for forty-two months.** These months add up to 3½ years. This was said above because the war of Heraclius against the Persians lasted for seven years—half of this ascribed to Chosroes and the other half to his son.

7. **Also it was allowed to make war on the saints** Because he killed St. Anastasius with seventy monks and many others.[2] **It was given authority over every tribe and people** Because many nations and diverse languages were under his power; this is a hyperbole, by taking every people and nation for many people and nations, just as it is frequently done in the Scripture and in everyday language. For it is regularly said that the whole city is at a feast to denote that there are many from the city there, and similarly it is added:

8. **And all the inhabitants of the earth will worship it . . . Everyone whose name has not been written . . . in the book of the life of the Lamb** That is, in the book of divine predestination, which is called the book of the life of the lamb by reason of the deity and also by reason of the humanity, insofar as all the predestined are saved in the faith of the mediator. **Who was slaughtered from the foundation of the world.** This is possible to be understood in two ways: in one way in a sense of preparation, because from eternity God disposed to create the world—which disposition can be called a certain foundation of the world, in relation to the exemplar of the world preconceived eternally by God, which was produced temporally in effect. As Boethius writes in the *Consolation*, "From the heavenly pattern you draw out all things bearing the world in your mind and forming it in

the same likeness."[3] It can be understood in another way figuratively. Thus from the beginning of the world Christ was sacrificed in Abel. For the killing of the innocent Abel was a figure of this Lamb, as Augustine says that he was slaughtered in Abel and exonerated among the prophets.[4]

9. Here at last, the end of the war between the Persians and Heraclius is described, when it is said: **Let anyone who has an ear** That is, understand. **Listen:** Supply the end of the war between Heraclius and the Persians, because the Persians who had led many Christians into captivity were themselves captured by Heraclius and his army. **If you kill with the sword,** Because Chosroes, who had killed many, was killed by Heraclius.

Here is a call for endurance . . . Because Zacharias, patriarch of Jerusalem, who with many other saints had been led into captivity, had the merit of endurance and was led back to Jerusalem by Heraclius.[5]

Muhammad

13:11 **Then I saw** Having described the persecution of Chosroes and his son, here the same is described under Muhammad and his people. It is divided into three parts. First, this persecution begins; second, it is interrupted by another, at the place, **Then I looked, and there was a white cloud,** (14:14); and third, the first part is resumed, at the place: **And the sixth angel** (16:12).[6]

The first section is divided in three parts, because first the situation of the Saracen sect is included; second the persecution of the Christians in the beginning of the following chapter; and third, the punishment of the persecutors, at the place: **"I saw another angel."** (14:8)

The first part is again in two parts, because first the situation of the sect is described; and second the veiling of a certain secret judgement, at the place: **This calls for wisdom:** (13:18). Concerning the first it should be known that, although the beginning of the sect of Muhammad is spoken of in various ways by various persons, nevertheless, it is more conveniently held that it began around the end of Heraclius's reign discussed in the preceding part.

Muhammad, elevated from poverty to wealth, intended to become the king of the Ishmaelites; for he belonged to this people, who are properly called the children of Hagar. Ishmael was the son of Hagar, the handmaid of Sarah (Gn 16); nevertheless, freed from Sarah, they are inappropriately called Saracens.[7] To obtain his goal, he used the counsel and help of a certain heretical monk, Sergius.[8] By writing a false and carnal law and having colored it with certain authorities from the Old and New Testaments, he was the more easily accepted, not only by Gentiles prone to carnal matters but also by simple Christians and Jews, who lived with the Ishmaelites. He also invented the fiction that this law was revealed by God to the greatest prophet of God.

Therefore, concerning him it is said: **Then I saw another beast** That is, Muhammad who was leading a licentious life, which is called bestial. For he was lecherous and afire with the ardor of lust for all persons of the eastern region, boasting singlehandedly to have God-given copulating and generative powers greater than forty men, as it is written in Book I, Chapter 5, of the *History of the Eastern Church,* which is otherwise called the book of James of Vitry, who is the author.[9]

Ascending Because through business and through rapine he ascended from poverty to riches, as is said in the same place. **It had two horns like a lamb** That is, of Christ, whose two horns are called prophecy, insofar as Christ was a wayfarer on earth and the proclaimer of the new law. (Lk declared in chapter 7:16 concerning this, "A great prophet has risen among us.") Muhammad imagined that he was a prophet and a giver of the divine law, as has been said. Therefore, it is said that he had two horns like the horns of a lamb, because they were not truthfully such, but according to human fiction. **And it spoke like a dragon.** Namely, cleverly, lyingly, and deceitfully.

12. **It exercises all the authority of the first beast** Some explain this concerning the sin of Chosroes, who was called the beast above. For Muhammad and his followers transferred the authority of the kingdom of the Persians to the Saracens, and thus it is said that he had all the authority of the first beast.

But what follows seems contrary to this exposition: **And it makes the earth . . .** By transferring the authority from the Persians, he did not make them adore their king, but much more to the contrary. On account of which it seems to me, and I submit myself to better judgement, that the first beast was himself Muhammad,[10] who is called a beast by reason of his bestiality, as was said. The first, because he was the first ruler of the Saracens, who were living in a bestial fashion. Moreover, it is the manner of the first ruler in any kingdom to firm up his control and to expand it as much as he is able, which Muhammad did. Therefore it says, **And it exercises all the authority . . .** Because whatever a first ruler is accustomed to do to firm up and expand his authority, he did the more diligently.

On its behalf, That is, as it seems expedient to a violent end for him.

And it makes the earth and all it inhabitants worship the first beast, That is, himself, who is called the first beast above, but he does not cause himself to be adored as God, as Chosroes did, but just as the highest prophet of God. **Whose mortal wound had been healed.** In a certain battle Muhammad was seriously wounded but was healed afterwards, as was said in the *History of the Eastern Church,* Chapter 5.[11]

13. **It performs great signs,** Nevertheless, false ones. **Even making fire come down from heaven** This fire is taken metaphorically, just as the other things which are mentioned here. For after Muhammad had a great effect, he began to fall into epileptic fits, and, lest he be despised, he said that he suffered this because of the appearance of the Archangel, Gabriel; a strong man is not able to bear his light, as Daniel said to the angel appearing to him, "My Lord because of the vision such pains have come upon me that I retain no strength" (Dn 10:16). Indeed, angels are called "fire" in Ps 104:4, "You make the winds your messengers, fire and flame your ministers." And because he was deceitful, therefore, it is added: **In the sight of all.** That is, in the erroneous opinion of those believing him. For his disciple said that he caused the moon to descend with his voice, which because of its light is associated with fire, and thus according to the opinion of people he made fire descend.

14. **And he deceives.** Through him and his disciples. **By the signs** Which are erroneously called such. **On behalf of the beast** That is, of himself; for they knew that the signs were deceitful or otherwise. **On behalf of the**

---

beast That is, of a bestial people, and easily seduced—the nature that the people of the Ishmaelites living in the desert were. **Telling the inhabitants of the earth** Subjected to him. **Telling them to make an image for the beast** This is added to designate that the beast is understood as Muhammad himself and not for the people deceived by him. Moreover, his image is called his law in which his nature and life are represented, which he ordered to be kept. And this is what is said: **To make an image** That is, that his law might be fulfilled.

15. **And it was allowed to give** That is, permission by God. **Breath to the image of the beast** That is, the vigor of his law. For the law is called life as long as it flourishes, and death when it is abrogated. **So that the image of the beast could even speak** That is, demonstrate his judgement, as it is said, "Such a law speaks concerning such a case." For nearly everything here is taken metaphorically. **And cause those who would not worship the beast to be killed.** For he commanded under pain of death that his law be kept in great reverence.

16. **Also it causes all, both small and great,** That is, all persons regardless of condition. **To be marked** That is, circumcision, as some say. For the Saracens are circumcised just as the Jews. But the following letter seems to disagree, when it says: **On the right hand** For circumcision was not done here. And therefore this mark seems to mean a determinate manner of living according to the law of Muhammad by which the Saracens are distinguished from other peoples. Therefore, it is said: **On the right hand** In relation to the operation. **Or on the forehead,** Through open confession.

17. **So that no one can buy or sell** That is, to take part with the Saracens in their laws. **Who does not have**

the mark, That is, the manner of living mentioned above. **That is, the name** False Saracens, as it were; for just as among Christians there are some who are false, on account of which they are allowed to communicate with true Christians, thus it is also true among the Saracens. **Or the number of its name.** The servants of the Saracens, as it were, of another law, who share with them in human concerns, because they are from the households of the Saracens.

18. **This calls for wisdom:** Here, the veiling of a certain secret judgement is included, namely, the number of Muhammad's years. Therefore, it is said: **This calls for wisdom:** That is, a hidden thing, which to grasp properly is wisdom. **Let anyone with understanding** That is, quick learning and the ability to penetrate secrets. **Calculate the number of the beast,** That is, of Muhammad who is called the beast, as was made clear earlier.

For it is the number That is, of a year. To what this number definitely refers is clear, and it does not refer to the number of years in his life, because he only flourished for sixty-three years, as *The Speculum of History* reports.[12] Therefore, some have said that it refers to the duration of his law, which ought to last that long; however, this does not seem true, because his law was given around the time of Heraclius, as was said above. Heraclius began to rule in the year of our Lord 613, and ruled for thirty years. Moreover, from the end of this to the present time, which is the year of our Lord 1329,[13] more time has passed, as is clear upon reflection, and, moreover, the law of Muhammad still endures.

Therefore, some say that after the death of Muhammad his law was corrected by the wise ones of the

Saracens, and from that reform one ought to begin counting the number of years of this law. But this does not seem probable, because this suggestion addresses the law not of Muhammad but of the wise ones. Besides, because these wise ones are said to have been disciples of Muhammad, and that reform was not long after the giving of the law by Muhammad, and from that time already 669 years have passed, the years are very nearly completed. Moreover, the law of Muhammad does not seem near an end but, in the last few years, has grown much stronger. For the Tartars, who are great in number, have accepted that law for a great part of their people, as I have heard asserted by a certain bishop of our order, who lived among the Tartars for many years.[14]

Therefore it seems, but I submit myself to better judgement, that this number of years is to begin from the incarnation of the Lord and to end with the death of Muhammad concerning whom John speaks prophetically.[15] This can be said, because from the year of the Incarnation of the Lord to the end of the reign of Heraclius 643 years passed, as was made evident before. Muhammad lived for sixty-three years, as has been said. Together these numbers make 706 years, from which it is necessary to subtract the years in which he flourished with Heraclius; otherwise they would be counted twice, as is clear by intuition. These years can probably be estimated to be forty, because Muhammad was first poor, and afterwards he grew strong through trade and rapine and fraud before he made himself king and made the law, which he gave at the death of Heraclius. Thus from the life of Muhammad it seems probable that sixty years had passed before the death of Heraclius, which [that is, forty] subtracted from

706 leaves precisely 666 remaining from the incarnation of the Lord to the death of Muhammad—according to this it is possible to explain it according to the letter. For the number is of a person, namely, Christ, who was a perfect human in knowledge and powers from the instance of the Incarnation.[16]

Its number. Of Muhammad, 666, because this number was from the year of the Lord's incarnation to the end of the life of Muhammad, as was said above. It should be known, moreover, that the book of the Apocalypse was written in Greek, in which the name is "Anthemos," when it is said 666 for which the meaning is, "contrary." This is appropriate for Muhammad, who was contrary to Christ by denying his divinity, as was said before and by persecuting the Christians, as will be said in the following section. Moreover, the significance of this word was applied to the number 666. To understand this, it should be known that just as in Latin some letters are applied to signify numbers—the letter "C" stands for one hundred and "L" for fifty and some for others—similarly in Greek, some letters are used for numbers. The name "Anthemos" written in Greek signifies 666 in Latin; therefore, in some Bibles the word "Diclvx" is used. **For it is the number of a person** This signifies among the Latins the name through letters in which it is written: the letter "D" for five hundred, "I" for one, "C" for one hundred, "L" for fifty, "V" for Five, and "X" for ten. Together this makes 666, which number coincides with Muhammad in a manner of speaking, because this is used very obscurely, as is clear, and therefore it is said: **This calls for wisdom.**

Notes

1. This story echoes Old Testament accounts in which heroes fight, instead of armies, for the freedom of their people, e.g., David and Goliath. Peter relates the same story, p. 501.

2. Alexander, p. 276, who cites the *Sächsische Weltchronik* and Frutolf-Ekkehard, 153, 11.

3. Boethius, *The Consolation of Philosophy*, Book 3, 9. See the Loeb Library edition for the complete text and translation. *Boethius: The Theological Tractates and the Consolation of Philosophy* (Cambridge, Mass.: Harvard University Press, 1973), p. 273.

4. Alexander, p. 277, who cites Haimo 1097; Jer 17:13.

5. Lyra devotes a major portion of the Commentary to the war between Heraclius and the Persians because the triumph of Heraclius was Christianity's first holy war, and Lyra could sanction this crusade.

6. He returns to the theme of Islam with the fifth angel in 16:10. Islam plays a major role in Nicholas's understanding of eschatology. He was not able to understand why God allowed Islam to be so successful in its advances against the Christians. In a lengthy response to Nicholas, included in almost all editions of Nicholas's Commentary, Paul of Burgos tried to explain the ways of God in relation to Islam's successes. See my essay, "Nicholas of Lyra and Paul of Burgos on Islam," in *Medieval Christian Perceptions of Islam: A Book of Essays*, ed. John Tolan (New York: Garland, 1996).

7. Another medieval etymology from John of Damascus calls them, "Sent empty away by Sarah."

8. Sergius, Patriarch of Constantinople (d. 638), was the most influential exponent of Monothelitism, a christological heresy in which one will and energy was emphasized in Christ. The doctrine of

two energies and two wills in Christ was established as orthodox over against monothelitism at the Council of Constantinople in 681.

9. Jacques de Vitry, *Historia orientalis,* ed. J Bongars (Douai, 1597), Book I, Ch. 5. James of Vitry (ca. 1160–1240) was an Augustinian Canon Regular known for his preaching and historiography. In 1216 he was consecrated bishop of Acre and also accompanied the army of the Fifth Crusade at Damietta (1218–21).

10. This is a classic Lyra step that can make reading the Commentary difficult. Earlier he had gone to great lengths to describe this first beast as the son of Chosroes, without any indication that he would retract it later because the text presents difficulties that he and his predecessors had not seen: i.e., that there is a positive relationship between the first and second beasts in the text that did not exist between the Persians and the Muslims. The Commentary seems to have developed in lectures and with different corrections, without editing earlier comments, as will become clearer.

11. Jacques de Vitry, *Historia orientalis*, Book I, Ch. 5.

12. Lyra frequently appeals to "textbook" answers such as that of Vincent of Beauvais's *Speculum Historiale* to qualify the interpretations of his models.

13. This reference provides the date for Lyra's final edition of this work.

14. Another source for Lyra's evidence seems to have been oral reports.

15. In Nicholas's understanding of history, John can see things prophetically that he cannot see as a human.

16. This comment is not clear except that 777 would be a perfect number and, therefore, its contrary would be 666.

Chapter 14
MUHAMMAD CONTINUED, ST BONIFACE, THE
LOMBARDS, THE CAROLINGIANS, AND CHARLEMAGNE

1. **Then I looked, and there was the Lamb,** Here the reward is described for those enduring the persecution of Muhammad, and it is divided in two parts, namely, in the principle and incidental, which begins at the place: **And I saw another angel** (14:6). Concerning the first, one should know that just as it was said in *The Chronicles* of Hugh of Fleury,[1] around the end of Heraclius' reign, the Hagareni, who are called Saracens with Muhammad as leader, began to invade Egypt and Ethiopia. Similarly, Omar, a disciple of Muhammad, occupied Damascus, the region of Phoenicia, Jerusalem, and all Syria, and he attacked Antioch. In these lands there were many Christian religious in large monasteries of two to three hundred or more monks living in chastity, of whom the greater part were virgins. In that persecution they were taken by the sword to the kingdom of heaven.

Then I looked, and there was the Lamb, That is, Christ, who is called the Lamb of God (Jn 1:29). **Standing on Mount Zion.** That is, in the Church triumphant, which is called Mount Zion in Heb 12:22, and is described here as standing, because it helped the martyrs through the unbearableness of martyrdom. In Acts 7:55, it is said that Stephen in the contest saw Jesus standing; because to stand is appropriate for battle; to sit indeed is proper for judging. Therefore, at the end of Mk [16:19], Jesus is described as sitting at the right hand of God. **And with him were one hundred forty-four thousand** Such a number or thereabouts was probably slain. **Who had his name and his Father's name** Through the Holy Spirit, who is the bond of both. **Written on their foreheads.** Through open and free confession.

2. **And I heard a voice from heaven like the sound of many ...** That is, of a multitude of saints according to which it is said in chapter 17:15, **"The many waters are peoples and multitudes."** For the multitude, the one hundred forty-four thousand, praise God mightily for his victory and for the glory which was obtained. **And like the sound of loud thunder;** This designates the magnitude of the praise, not only out of the multitude of those praising but also the manner and the quality of praise. **The voice I heard was like the sound of harpists playing on their harps.** This praise is before God and pleasing to the angels.

3. **And they sing a new song** Because those who are praising are from the number of saints of the New Covenant. **Before the Throne** Of God. **And before the four living creatures** That is, in the presence of the holy patriarchs and bishops existing in heaven, just as it was said in the fourth chapter. **No one could learn that song** For on account of the vow of continence, they possessed something special in merit and similarly in reward, as the Church sings concerning any holy witness, "None is found like him" By reason of special merit. **Who have been redeemed from the earth.** By the blood of Christ.

4. **It is these who have not been defiled with women,** By keeping the purity of the body, or at least after the vow, preserving chastity. **For they are virgins.** In the Scripture, virginity is sometimes taken strictly for the purity of the body, sometimes more broadly for continence, especially, after a consecrated vow. **These**

follow the Lamb wherever he goes. Because they follow the way of Christ not only by way of the commands but also of the counsels. **They have been redeemed from humankind as first fruits for God.** . . . That is, pleasing, as the first fruits are the more delectable.

5. **And in their mouth no lie was found.** For they confessed the truth of the faith entirely and constantly. **They are blameless before the throne of God.** For if they had committed any sin, it was purged by virtue of their martyrdom.

6. **Then I saw another angel** This is the incidental part, in which a certain marvelous conversion of unbelievers is described, which occurred at that time. For St. Boniface was sent by the Roman pontiff to proclaim the catholic faith to the Gentiles of Thuringia, Austria, and Frisia. In this mission he converted many to Christ, and this is what is said: **Then I saw another angel** That is, St. Boniface; for angel means messenger. Thus he was the messenger of the word of God, as was said. **Flying in mid heaven,** For he speedily and promptly accomplished the assignment given him. **Having** In his heart and mouth. **The eternal gospel** That is, the Gospel of Christ, which is called eternal, for nothing else will succeed it.[2] **To proclaim to those who live on the earth**—That is, to these people among whom languages are different, at least in relation to one another. Because he was prepared to preach not only to these people but also generally to all nations wishing to hear him; therefore, it is added: **To every nation and tribe.** . . .

7. **He said in a loud voice,** In this one notes the effects of his preaching. **"Fear God"** With filial fear. **"And give him glory,"** As sons to a father. **"For the**

hour of his judgement has come;" Generally at the end of the world but for each person at death. In such a status the person who dies will be presented for judgement, **"And worship him . . ."** Who is the creator of all and not vain idols.

8. **Then another angel,** Here he describes the punishment of those who persecute the Christians. And it is divided into two parts, because first he describes their punishment; and second the occasion of the reward of the good, at the place: **And I heard a voice** (14:13).

Concerning the first, it should be known that Constans, the nephew of Heraclius, began to rule in the year of our Lord 644 and persuaded by Paul, bishop of Constantinople, he fell into the Monothelite heresy, denying two natures in Christ. He grievously persecuted many ministers of the Church who did not assent to this heresy and sent them into exile. Therefore, St. Martin, the pope, having convened a council, condemned this heresy with its followers. Therefore, he was taken to Constantinople to assent to this heresy, but refusing he was sent into exile, where he died. This is how some interpret this, when it is said: **Then another angel,** That is, Pope Martin. **Followed saying,** By condemning this heresy **"Fallen, fallen is Babylon"** That is, the empire of the Greeks, which was great; for after the emperor fell into heresy, as was said, many others similarly fell. And because it was "confused," that empire was called Babylon; that is, "confused." Moreover, **"Fallen"** is said twice, because of two falls, namely of the patriarch and of the emperor.

Therefore, one should know that it is said in the *Chronicle* of Sigebert that Leo, who assumed the reign after Theodosius, began to rule in the year of the Lord 718, and he ruled for twenty-four years, and in the thirteenth year of his reign Pope Gregory III presided over the Church. He rebuked Leo, who was corrupted by heresy, and refused him the income of the Romans, and lest one coin struck with his image be received, he commanded that his effigy be taken from the church lest his name be recited in the solemn Mass.[3] This is how this is explained by them because it is added:

9. **Then another angel, a third,** That is, Pope Gregory. **Followed them, crying with a loud voice,** This notes the authority of his ordination. **"Those who worship the beast"** That is, Leo, living like the beast by handing over the honor of the empire to him. **"And its image,"** Which he had removed from the Church, as was said. **"And receive a mark . . ."** By clearly acknowledging him as emperor. **"Or on their hands,"** By accepting a coin imprinted with his image.

10. **"They will also drink the wine of God's wrath,"** By incurring the punishment of excommunication. Nevertheless, although this exposition seems probable, because before the Emperor Constans there were other emperors who were corrupted by heresy as much as, if not more [than Leo III], as was said above. Therefore, this exposition seems less convenient,[4] because it was said above concerning the fall, **"Fallen, fallen is Babylon"** That is, the rule of the Greeks, especially since his son Constantine repaired the disrupted churches[5] and rose up against the heresy of the Monothelites. Whereupon he gathered a universal synod in Constantinople of 289 bishops, who approved and demonstrated that there were two natures in the Lord Jesus Christ.[6] Similarly,

because it adds the issues of Pope Gregory and Emperor Leo and his coin. **"They will also drink the wine of God's wrath,"** By incurring excommunication.

It seems to be less convenient, because it is added: **"And they will be tormented with fire and sulfur"** Through this the punishment of hell seems to be meant, which is eternal, when it is added: **"And the smoke of their torment goes up. . . ."** This does not seem to address the punishment of excommunication, or of the burning of his body, which they say happened to Constantine, the son of Leo, who was the greatest persecutor of the ministers of the Church. Therefore (submitting myself to better judgement), it seems that the text from that place: **Then another angel, a second,** (14:8) should be explained concerning Muhammad and his followers whose persecution against the Church he had mentioned but had not yet spoken of their punishment. Therefore, here John describes their punishment: first, in relation to temporal punishment; second, to eternal punishment, at the place: **Then another angel, a third,** (14:9).[7]

Concerning the first he says: **The angel** Namely, St. John speaking. **Followed** This does not refer to the part immediately preceding, but to the part in which he had spoken concerning the 144,000 killed for Christ by the Saracens (14:1) and speaking of their temporal punishment. **"Fallen, fallen is Babylon"** (14:8) This is the people of Babylon; for his law is filled with confusions, because the licentious life was let loose there and also because of the law's confusing way of progressing; for it is related in a disordered fashion, and similarly repeats itself frequently and uselessly. Nor is it supported by reason or Scripture, as is clear by intuition. **"The great!"**

(14:8) For in a short time this people multiplied and spread out greatly. Moreover, it is said: **"Fallen"** Because around that time this people fought with the Romans, in which conflict three divisions of the Saracens with many others were destroyed, as is reported in the Chronicle of Sigebert.[8] **"She has made all nations drink of the wine of the wrath of her fornication."** This is hyperbole to designate the great multitude of the gentiles infected by the error of Muhammad. For he allows the delights of the flesh to which most of humanity is prone.

Then the third angel (14:9) Here their eternal punishment is described, when it is said: **The third angel** Evidently according to the letter; or some holy preacher against the sect of Muhammad. **"Those who worship the beast"** That is, Muhammad, as was said in the preceding chapter where his image and the reception of his mark are discussed. **"They will also drink the wine of God's wrath,"** (14:10) The sect will be grievously punished by God. **"Poured unmixed into the cup of his anger."** Moreover, the punishment of God is called "unmixed wine" when someone is punished for temporal correction; "mixed" indeed when after the temporal the eternal follows, as in the case in question, because the Saracens were punished by temporal death, as has been said, and eternal death. Therefore, it is added: **"And they will be tormented with fire and sulfur"** That is, the punishment of Gehenna.

11. **"And the smoke of their torment"** This is the eternal punishment afterwards. **"There is no rest day or night"** For it is continuous as is clear from the preceding chapter. And according to what St. Augustine says: One cause why evil persons are permitted in this world is for

the training of the good in the virtue of patience.[9] Therefore, it is added:

12. **Here is a call for the endurance of the saints,** Because the patience of Christians was oftentimes and in many ways tested by the Saracens.

13. **And I heard** By some this part is explained by the death with which one dies to the world upon entering the religious life. In these times a certain powerful man, having been led by devotion, rebuilt the monastery of St. Benedict in Monte Cassino, which had been destroyed for many years before by the Lombards, and serving there by example he led many to the service of Christ. At this time many nobles from various regions, having left the pomp of the world to serve Christ and assuming the religious habit, had died to the world—because of this it is said about them: **"Blessed are the dead"** Also because it is added: **"Yes," says the Spirit, "they will rest from their labors"** For they cross from the work of the active life to the rest of the contemplative, but while dying to the world they are not dying to the Lord properly speaking, but they begin to live the more in him; nor do they rest from their work, but assume it the more by the love of Christ: namely, vigils, prayers, fasts, and the like.

Therefore, it seems better to say that here, after the eternal punishment of the evil, the eternal reward of the good is described, as was said above, so that they may shine the more with these opposites having been placed alongside them. Therefore, it is said to John here: **"Write this:"** As if a most notable thing. **"Blessed are the dead who die in the Lord."** That is, in the confession of our Lord Jesus Christ through the martyr's crown, such as the 144,000 mentioned in the previous chapter. **"Yes," says**

---

the Spirit, Namely, the Holy Spirit, who with the Father and the Son is one God. He is mentioned here specifically; for works are meritorious through love, through which the Holy Spirit dwells in us, and thus the reward is in a certain way specifically attributed to him. **"They will rest from their labors,"** In beatitude the appetite is totally at rest. **"For their deeds"** The merits for eternal life. **"Follow them."** In the beatitude which they will receive for them.

14. **Then I looked,** The persecution of the Saracens having been begun, here other persecutions, namely of the Lombards, are interspersed. This is done on account of the succession of time, which order John follows in this book.[10] It is divided into two parts: first, the liberation of the Church from the Lombards is described; and second, the striking of many others persecuting it, at the place: **After this I looked,** (15:5).

Concerning the first it should be known that in the year of our Lord 753, Aistulf, king of the Lombards, greatly afflicted the Church in Italy, so that Steven travelled to the Frankish kingdom seeking help against this king, which he obtained, and this is described in this part. Moreover, it is divided in two parts because first the aid at the time of Pepin is described; and second, at the time of his son, Charlemagne, at the place: **Another angel** (14:15). Concerning the first, it is said: **Then I looked, and there was a white cloud,** Here the king of the Franks is understood made white from previous customs and by faith. **Seated on the cloud** King Pepin. **One like the Son of Man,** Having been conformed to Christ in faith and in justice, although this assimilation was over a long time. **With a golden crown on his head,** For the kings of the

Franks were literally crowned with a golden crown. **And in his hand** That is, by his power. **A sharp sickle!** That is, an exercise of arms through which Pepin was often and greatly victorious.

15. **Another angel** That is, Pope Steven. **Came out of the temple,** Of the Roman Church. **Calling with a loud voice** That is, interceding out of great love. **To the one who sat on the cloud,** That is, King Pepin. **"Use your sickle and reap,"** By directing the power of your army against the tyrant, Aistulf. **"For the hour to reap has come,"** That is, his tyranny should be destroyed by your power, **"Because the harvest of the earth is fully ripe."** That is, he and his army were stubborn in their iniquity.

16. **So the one who sat on the cloud swung his sickle over the earth,** With a strong hand, Pepin invaded Italy and reaped the earth, because he fought vigorously against Aistulf and forced him to return to St. Peter whatever belonged to its jurisdiction.

17. **Then another angel** Here the help for the Church against the Lombards is described at the time of Charlemagne. It is divided into two parts, because first the help of Charlemagne is included; and second the expansion of the divine worship in the subsequent chapter.

Concerning the first, it should be known that in the year of our Lord 775 at the request of Pope Adrian, Charlemagne, king of the Franks, invaded Italy with a mighty army against Desiderius, king of the Lombards, who was afflicting the Church in many ways. After defeating him he led him in exile to the kingdom of the Franks and made Lombardy a part of his kingdom, and this is what is said here: **And another angel** Namely,

Charlemagne. **Came out of the temple** In which he was crowned, as is reported in the *Chronicle of Sigebert.*[11] **In heaven,** Of the Church militant, which is frequently called "heaven" in the Scripture. **And he too had a sharp sickle.** That is, a strong army, indeed stronger than his father's.

18. **Then another angel** That is, Pope Adrian. **Came out from the altar,** Which he had approached to celebrate the Mass so that God would protect the Church. **The angel who has authority over fire,** That is, to carry out excommunication and grievous punishment.[12] For any punishment is sometimes designated by the name of fire. Some books have **And water,** But this is not from the text, nor is it in the corrected books.[13] **And he called with a loud voice** With great love, asking Charlemagne to help him. **"Use your sharp sickle"** That is, the power of your army. **"And gather the clusters"** That is, the Lombards, by removing their power. **"For its grapes are ripe."** That is, the Lombards are worthy of destruction.

19. **So the angel swung** That is, Charlemagne. **His sickle** That is, the power of his army. Some books have **"Sharp" [sickle] over the earth** but this is not in the text.[14] **And gathered the vintage of the earth,** By taking the power of the Lombards from Italy. **And threw it into the great wine press of the wrath of God.** For he led the king into captivity.

20. **And the wine press was trodden outside the city,** Because he led the king and his wife outside his land, as has been said. **And the blood flowed from the wine press,** During the capture of the king, many Lombards were killed. **As high as a horse's bridle,** The blood of those killed made the bridles of the soldiers of

Charles red, as it occurs in such wars. **For a distance of about 1600** *stadia.* The report of Charles's victory was spread far and wide, namely, through the four parts of the world designated by this number. It is a squared number which is the product of a number multiplied by itself. Just as four is a product of two times itself: two times two is four. Similarly, nine is a product of three: three times three is nine. Such is the case here; for 1600 is the produce of forty times itself: forty times forty is 1600. It is clear—the number above represents the four parts of the world.

Notes

1. Hugh of Fleury, *Historia Ecclesiastica, PL* 163. The Benedictine priest, Hugh, a biographer and historian who died after 1118, wrote his *Historia Ecclesiastica* (1109) covering the period to 855 and added a chronicle of the kings of France, covering the period from 842–1108.

2. Like Alexander and Peter, Nicholas identifies this angel with St. Boniface. The Gospel is called eternal because nothing succeeds it. Peter and Nicholas are eager to agree with this interpretation over against a radical Franciscan interpretation, which had interpreted Joachim of Fiore's prophecies of the Third Status to indicate that leadership in the Church would pass to the Franciscans. The Third Status would supersede the Two Testaments. The Franciscan Gerard of Borgo San Donnino, for example, caused a stir in 1254 in Paris with these ideas (see the introduction).

3. Sigebert of Gembloux, *Chronicon,* Monumenta Germaniae Scriptorum (Hanover, 1844), 6:330 [henceforth, MGH. SS]. Sigebert—teacher, hagiographer, and historian (1030–1112)— flourished during the thirty years in which the investiture struggle was

at its height. In a letter to Pope Paschal II (1103), he charged Pope Gregory VII with producing many ills by his innovations, and he supported royal and imperial investiture against usurping popes.

4. This is an example of how complicated Nicholas's scholastic commentary could become. He has finished narrating a whole section and now objects to it and will pose another alternative.

5. Constantine IV; for a discussion of his reforms see George Ostrogorsky, *History of the Byzantine State* (New Brunswick, N.J.: Rutgers University Press, 1969), pp. 123–30.

6. The Sixth Ecumenical Council, November 680 to September 681.

7. Nicholas is always careful to avoid assigning emperors the role of evil figures in the Commentary unless he is forced to do so by history or the text. Here he disagrees with both Alexander and Peter and chooses an antagonist outside the *corpus christianum.*

8. Sigebert of Gembloux (1030–1112). See note 3 above.

9. I was not able to locate this citation.

10. This is the interruption in the theme of Islam that Nicholas promised at 13:11.

11. MGH. SS. 6:336.

12. Here Peter Auriol explains that the passage refers to the pope's plenitude of power: the fire referring to the pope's plenitude of power *in foro exteriori* (the external forum) of excommunicating and sentencing; the water referring to his power *in foro interiori* (the internal forum) of freeing the conscience through the sacraments. Nicholas is very general and is careful not to attribute to the pope more powers than necessary. He even quarrels with the biblical text at this point, undermining Peter's interpretation. Alexander's interpretation is more general, like that of Nicholas.

---

13. This is an interesting note of textual criticism.

14. For a discussion of the various university texts available in Paris see Ralph Loewe, "The Medieval History of the Latin Vulgate," in *The Cambridge History of the Bible: The West, From The Fathers to The Reformation*, vol. 2, ed. G. W. H. Lampe (Cambridge: Cambridge University Press, 1969), pp. 148ff. See also Margaret T. Gibson, *The Bible in the Latin West* (Notre Dame: University of Notre Dame Press, 1993), pp. 10ff.

Chapter 15
THE PERSECUTORS OF THE CHURCH ARE PERSECUTED

1. **Then I saw another portent** After the description of the destruction of the Lombards, the persecution of more persecutors of the Church is described. It is divided into two parts: first this persecution is described; and second the execution of the persecution, at the place: **After this I looked,** (15:5) The first is in two parts, because first this persecution is described; second the divine praise, on account of this, at the place: **And I saw** (15:2).

Concerning the first it is said: **Then I saw another portent** It was the sign of a future event. **Great and amazing:** For the persecutions of the enemies of the Church were signified through this, namely, the enemies who had been destroyed by the power of God. **Seven angels** These are individually treated in the following chapter. **With seven plagues,** That is, the power of inflicting them from God. **Which are the last,** Not simply, but in respect to past time, just as in Gn 49:1 it is said, "Gather around, that I may tell you what will happen to you in days to come." Nevertheless, these were already completed for a long time. **For with them the wrath of God is ended.** That is, through these the vengeance of God has been set for the reprobate in effect. For wrath is the desire for vengeance which is consumed when it occurs in effect.

2. **And I saw what appeared to be a sea** Here the divine praise is described which followed the persecutions of the reprobate; nevertheless here its execution is set immediately in advance. Frequently in Scripture events are placed earlier, because the saints in heaven seeing these persecutions spoke before they occurred in effect. Therefore, John says: **And I saw what appeared to be a sea** That is, the Church militant, which is called such because of baptism, as was said above in the fourth chapter. **Mixed with fire,** Of the Holy Spirit, which is given in baptism. **And those who had conquered the beast** That is, the Saracen people designated here by the beast, because Muhammad, whose heresy they hold, is called such in chapter 13. **And its image** That is, resembling the Saracens. **And the number of its name,** That is, following the Saracens, or by the number of its name one should understand the infidels who are in every way contrary to Christ and the Church. For the name of its number noted above was *anthemos,* for which the principle meaning is "contrary," namely, to Christ (see end of chapter 13). Moreover, the seven plagues—the next persecutions—are on the Saracens, or on those like them, or on those contrary to Christ and to the Church, as will be clear below. . . . [1]

1. The rest of chapter 15 is redundant, so I have omitted the translation. Nevertheless, a new division of history begins in that the persecutors of the Church are punished.

Chapter 16

The Iconoclastic Controversy, The Power and Glorious Accomplishments of Charlemagne, and The First Crusade

1. **Then I heard** Having described the introduction to the seven plagues, here their execution is described; first in general, when it is said: **Then I heard a loud voice** Of which the magnitude of the divine authority is noted. **From the temple** Namely, of the glory of God. **Telling the seven angels,** To execute the divine commands to punish the reprobate. **"Go out,"** Here the execution is described specifically, and it is able to be divided into two parts, according to the number of the seven plagues, which will be clear by proceeding.

Concerning the first, one should know that Constantine, who began to rule in the year of the Lord 740, was wicked.[1] For as Sigebert says, he removed the images of Christ and the saints from the churches, and in many ways he tormented those who called on the Mother of God; those who conducted vigils in the churches; those who abstained from oaths and unclean things and deprived them of their property.[2] He also forced monks to marry, and, because many refused, they were martyred by him. After this with the support of Irene, the wife of Leo, ruling with his son Constantine, whose rule began in the year of the Lord 782, Pope Adrian called a council at the insistence of the patriarch of Constantinople in which he condemned the heresy denigrating the images of Christ and of the saints.[3] They are the books of the laity moving them to piety. Whence it is said that St. Luke was the first to have painted the images of Christ and the Blessed Virgin Mary.

He also condemned the heresy of Felix [of Urgel],[4] which placed a twofold filiation of God in Christ, namely a true one in the divine nature and an adopted one in the human. According to which it follows that a twofold person is in Christ, one in the divine nature, the other in the human, just as Nestorius said. Therefore, it follows that the Blessed Virgin was not the Mother of God, but only of the man. Indeed, these heresies have a similarity with the perfidy of Muhammad, for the Saracens despise images, and also say that Jesus, the son of Mary, the virgin, was pure man. Therefore, concerning the condemnation of this twofold heresy it is said:

2. **So the first angel went out** That is, Pope Adrian, who was holy and good. **And poured his bowl on the earth,** By excommunicating the earthly men holding these heresies. **And a foul and painful sore came** For excommunication (which is a spiritual plague) is worse than temporal punishment among the obstinate. **On those who had the mark of the beast** That is, the similarity to Muhammad described in the manner above. **And who worshipped its image.** By revering leaders similar to Muhammad.

3. **The second angel** Here the second plague is described, concerning which one should know that some

Roman citizens conspired against Pope Leo (who presided over the Church in the fifth year of Irene and of her son, Constantine). They cut his tongue twice and dug out his eyes and left him as if half-dead wallowing in his blood. Concerning this, some interpret the text to say that the Roman citizen who led others to this outrage is called the second angel who poured his bowl into the sea; that is, the Church is called the sea representing baptism. This citizen poured his malice and anger on the pope, who was the head of the Church. . . .[5]

But this does not seem to be reasonable, because it was clear earlier that the seven angels represent seven catholic and holy men; but this Roman citizen was wicked. Similarly, because it is added: **And every living thing in the sea died.** This does not agree with what has been said, because other than Pope Leo no one from the Church was harmed; this was a personal persecution.[6]

Therefore, it can be explained otherwise and better, as it seems, by Charlemagne, king of the Franks, who fought with the Saxons at this time. Here the sea designates the multitude of this people, as a manner of speaking, which is said in the following chapter: **"The waters are many peoples."** The sea is a gathering of much water. Similarly, because the Saxons navigating the sea afflicted many Christian lands, John says: **The second angel** Namely, Charlemagne, who was devoted to God and to the Church. **Poured his bowl into the sea,** By waging the divine vengeance on the Saxons. **And it became like the blood of a corpse,** Because many of the Saxons were killed, and because the remaining, seeing that Charlemagne was victorious by the power of God, accepted baptism; therefore it is not said: **And it became the blood**

of a corpse, simply, but: **"like" the blood of a corpse.**
The rest who were obstinate were killed. On one day,
Charlemagne had 4,500 beheaded; therefore it is added:
And every living thing in the sea died. . . .[7]

4. **The third angel** This is the third part, which is
similarly explained with reference to Charlemagne.
Having been made emperor twice he is called here an
angel, namely, the second and the third in the same way
as in 1 Sam. 10:9 when Saul is made king, because he was
changed into another man. Charles ruled over the Franks
for thirty years, and afterwards he was made emperor for
thirty years as is recorded in the *Chronicle of Sigebert.*[8] In
the third year of his reign he totally subdued the Mauros,
also called the Huns, who had ravaged many Christian
lands. Those who remained he subjected to the catholic
faith; therefore, it is added: **And the third** Namely, an
angered Emperor Charles. **Poured his bowl** That is, the
vengeance of God. **Into the rivers** That is, on the Mauros
or the Huns, as they are called, because they originally
lived near the swamps of Moesia where there is much
bubbling water like springs. These swamps were earlier
thought to be impossible to cross, but the Huns crossed
them and subdued the Goths who lived beyond these
swamps in Scythia. Lifted up by this victory they
devastated other lands by fire and sword as far as Gaul
under Attila their king. **And they became blood.** Because
the army of Charles killed many Huns.

5. **And I heard** To understand this one should know
that good angels who are from the rank of leaders rule
over diverse kingdoms and peoples, and therefore they
bring about the good of the people committed to them, on
account of which they seem to oppose one another when

things happen contrary to the people committed to them before they know the will of God for the people subjugated to them. In this way in Dn 10:13 Gabriel said to Daniel, "The prince of the kingdom of Persia opposed me for twenty-one days," as was exposited there at greater length. But when they know the divine will through revelation or the effect, they approve of the divine judgement. Their will always agrees with that of the divine will and according to this it is said: **And I heard the angel of the waters,** That is, of the Huns which is signified by the springs and rivers, as was said. **Saying, "You are just,"** By approving the divine sentence concerning the conquered people committed to him.

6. **"Because they shed the blood of saints and prophets,"** For before they were subdued by Charles, the Huns killed many Christians among whom some were endowed with sanctity and the gift of prophecy. **"You have given them blood to drink."** By fitting the punishment to the crime, as it is said commonly concerning punishment: He drinks with the same cup as he had others drink.

7. **And I heard the altar** Namely, the angel of the Franks. **Respond, "Yes, Oh Lord God,"** For both angels approved the divine sentence.

8. **The fourth angel** Here the fourth plague is described, which some expound with reference to a certain man called Crescentius, who as a Roman patrician should have protected the Church, but, on the contrary, he attacked it by deposing Pope Gregory, and in his place he put a certain man of little or no merit, John. Accordingly, it is said here that the fourth angel is Crescentius.[9] **Poured his bowl** That is, indignation and wrath. **On the sun,** That

is, on Pope Gregory, the vicar of Christ, holding the place of the sun of justice.

But this is not explained correctly, because, as it was said above, the angels are understood to be seven just and holy men; but Crescentius was evil, and therefore it is interpreted better by Pope Leo, who, having his sight and speech restored to him providentially, sent a legate to Charles asking his aid, and therefore it is said: **And the fourth angel** That is, the good and holy Pope Leo as is clear from what has been said. **Poured** By reporting the harm done to his spirit to Emperor Charles, because it was unjust and in contempt of God that he had been blinded and deprived of his tongue and deposed from Peter's see. Moreover, Charles is called the sun because just as the sun excels the other planets, Charles, gleaming in magnanimity and faith, excelled all other earthly kings. **And it was allowed to scorch them with fire.** Having been given the power by God he helped Rome, investigated the causes, afflicted and punished grievously the rebels against God and the Church, and restored Pope Leo to his see, as is reported in the *Chronicle* of Sigebert.[10]

9. **They were scorched** Namely, the wicked ones. **By the fierce heat,** Of anguish and of wrath because they were not able to resist Charles. **But they cursed the name of God,** This is said in relation to the obstinate ones, who died in their sins.

10. **The fifth angel** Here the fifth plague is described in which John returns to the persecution of the Saracens and their punishment, as has been said above.[11] Nevertheless, some explain this part as referring to Emperor Otto, who, as they say, restored Pope Gregory, who had been deposed by Crescentius, to the papacy by expelling

the intruder, John, and therefore it is said here: **The fifth angle** That is, Otto. **Poured his bowl on the throne of the beast,** That is, of the intruder, Pope John, living the life of a beast. But because earlier the beast was understood to be Muhammad, this part seems to be explained better with reference to the Saracens. Concerning this one should know, as Helinand says, that the patriarch of Jerusalem, who had been expelled from the city, sought help from Emperor Charles by reporting that his holy land had been torn asunder.[12] Gathering a larger army than he ever had before, Charles helped the Holy Land; the infidels were in part killed, and in part they fled. He restored the patriarch to his see and restored the Holy Land to the Christians in a good condition.[13] According to this it is said, **The fifth angel** That is, the Patriarch of Jerusalem. **Poured his bowl,** That is, the Emperor Charles, who was an instrument of God to punish the people of Muhammad; therefore it is added: **On the throne of the beast,** Moreover, here it is said that the patriarch of Jerusalem had poured this bowl, because he caused Charles to punish their contempt of God and the Church. **And its kingdom** Namely, of Muhammad. **Was plunged into darkness;** Because the Saracens were partly killed and partly expelled in a confused state from the holy land. **People gnawed their tongues in agony,** For it is the manner of an angered and afflicted person to chew on the lips and to gnash with the teeth as if eating the tongue.

11. **And cursed the God of heaven** Tormented by excessive impatience. **The God of heaven** That is, Christ, who is true God of heaven and earth. Nevertheless, the Saracens say that he was mere man, and thus they

blasphemed him. **And they did not repent of their deeds.** Stubborn in their perfidy.

12. **The sixth angel** Here the sixth plague is described. Some expound this part in relation to Pope Gregory, who was first called Hildebrand and presided over the Church at the time of Henry IV, who began to rule in the year of the Lord 1057. A conflict arose between him and Pope Gregory because Pope Gregory excommunicated all who were elected in the Church, who accepted investiture through the ring and staff from the hand of any lay person, since emperors and princes still used this power; thus they explain this passage: **The sixth angel** That is, Pope Gregory. **Poured his bowl** That is, indignation. **On the great river Euphrates,** That is, on the Roman Empire, which is called a great river, because of the magnitude of the number of people subjected to it, whence it is said in the following chapter (17:15), **"The waters are peoples and multitudes."** It is also called the Euphrates because it is the fourth kingdom, which is called "iron" in Dn 2:40–41, just as the Euphrates is the fourth river of Paradise (Gn 2:14). **And its water was dried up** By removing the power of investing in relation to those elected in this manner. **To prepare the way for the kings from the east. . . .** So that the elected, who are called kings because they have to rule the Church, are able freely to enter the churches. They are also called kings of the sun, because they are vicars of Christ, the sun of justice, in their dioceses, as the pope is in the universal Church.

This can be expounded in another way and more properly according to the letter, as it seems, concerning Charlemagne, who, invited by St. James, purged the way to his unknown sepulchre.[14] All of Spain was occupied by the Saracens to Vasconia and Navarre, and with enormous effort and battles Charles killed some; some fled; others he subjected to Christianity—by vexation he offered them understanding. This then is what is said: **The sixth angel** That is, St. James. **Poured his bowl** The power of Charlemagne, which St. James had invited to punish the Saracen people, which is called a great river due to the multitude of the people. **And its water was dried up** By taking away the Saracen power. **To prepare the way for the kings** That is, for pilgrims of St. James among whom frequently were and are many kings, princes and potentates. Therefore, Charles himself helped this shrine by his piety. And other pilgrims are also able to be called kings, because they live by the rule of the law of God and of right reason. **From the East. . . .** The grave of St. James is in the west of habitable land and therefore the way to it is from the rising of the sun—in relation to those who come from the East. . . .

13. **And I saw** Here the seventh plague is described, of which, first, the reason is introduced; and second, its execution, at the place: **The seventh angel** (16:17) Concerning the first, one should know that from the time of Chosroes, king of the Persians, for the most part, catholic people living in and around the Promised Land were in affliction and in harsh servitude until their liberation by the western Christian princes at the time of Godfrey of Bouillon, duke of Lorraine. The other liberations of these people by Heraclius and Charlemagne discussed earlier were short-lived; they quickly passed away. After Heraclius withdrew from Jerusalem having killed Chosroes and recapturing the Holy Cross, the Arabs, with Omar as

leader, subjugated the Holy Land and many others.[15] Similarly, after the withdrawal of Charlemagne from the Holy Land, the Saracens ruling in Egypt subjugated Judea to themselves. The Turks, taking it from the hand of the caliph, later held it until they were defeated by the princes noted above in parts of Antioch. After the power of the Turks was weakened, the Egyptians took Jerusalem and Judea from their hands, as the bishop of Tyre reports in Book 7, Chap. 12.[16] Within a year or more, the Christians took it from the hands of the Egyptians by force of arms. It should be noted also that among the Christians there were preachers exciting others to fight the Saracens, just as among the Saracens there were some learned who were exciting others against the Christians, which John foreseeing said: **And I saw from the mouth of the dragon,** That is, of the highest leader in the kingdom of Persia, who is called a dragon as in chapter 12 above. **From the mouth of the beast,** That is, of the caliph or of the highest leader in Egypt. **And from the mouth of the false prophet.** That is, of the preachers exciting the Saracens against the Christians, and here the singular is used for the plural, namely, "of the prophet" for "of the prophets," as is frequently done in Scripture. **And I saw three foul spirits** The words of these prophets and also of the leaders are called unclean spirits, because of the uncleanliness of sin. **Like frogs** For by their croaking they annoy others.

14. **These are demonic spirits,** Because the demons instigate this. **Performing signs,** For among the infidels demons are permitted to do some signs, although they are hidden to us. **Who go abroad to the kings of the whole world,** In which these infidels live, and they are called kings, satraps, potentates, and others established under the

leading princes. **To assemble them for battle** Some expositors say here that around the year 1066, Saracens both from Egypt and from other regions across the sea had gathered to devastate the Christian people, not only in Judea but also in Greece. But this does not seem true, because according to Bishop James of Vitry and also William of Tyre in the books which he wrote, the *History of Deeds Done Beyond the Sea*, after the death of Muhammad the Saracens were divided into two sects; one sect established its seat in Egypt, the other in the kingdom of Persia.[17] They were divided not only in location but also in certain points of their law; thus they call one another betrayers and schismatics. Therefore, among them there was contention and war to the time of Saladin, who began to rule in the year of the Lord 1180 after the long liberation of the Holy Land by these princes. Saladin persuaded the Saracens living in Egypt to hold the ceremonies of the others existing in Persia, and thus he returned them to concord; neither before nor after their division is it held in any noteworthy history that they gathered in one army against the Christian people.[18] Therefore what is said here: **To assemble them for battle** is not to be understood at the same time with respect to all, but successively as it was said above. **On the great day of God the Almighty.** Who by these gatherings of the infidels at various times punished the sins of the Christians, as the previously mentioned bishops say, whence it is added:

15. **"See I am coming like a thief!"** Such punishments the Lord unexpectedly sets on sinners sleeping in their impiety; therefore it is added: **"Blessed is the one who stays awake"** By attending to divine justice. **"And**

keeps his robes," Namely, of the virtues. **"Not going about naked . . ."** For one is stripped of the virtues through mortal sin. **"And exposed to shame."** Seen by God and the angels. 16. **And they assembled them** Successively, in the way noted earlier. **At the place that in Hebrew is called Harmagedon.** Jerome interprets this as "A rising up." In the land of promise Christ suffered and rose. 17. **The seventh angel** Here the persecution of the seventh plague is described, first in general and, second, more specifically in the following chapter. Concerning the first, one should know that some expositors say that this seventh angel was Alexius, the emperor of Constantinople, who wrote a letter to Pope Urban for the recovery of the Holy Land, but this does not seem true, because this Alexius was deceptive and deceitful towards the Latins and schemed in many ways to destroy the army of the western princes who were proceeding devoutly for that recovery. Thus the Lord Bishop of Tyre describes, and others more carefully describe, that pilgrimage.[19]

Therefore, it should be said that this angel was Peter the Hermit, born in the diocese of Amiens, who, moved by piety with great labor and dangers, went across the sea to visit the holy places.[20] When he had entered Jerusalem, having paid tribute to the Turks ruling there, he remained for some days with the patriarch and other catholics living in the city. Therefore, not only by their reports but also as an eyewitness, he understood the miseries of the Christian people—in the city and also in other places of Judea. Having compassion on them he said to them that they could have a remedy if they wrote an appeal to the supreme pontiff, who was able to exhort the faithful to this, and he also offered to carry their letter. Thanking him they committed their business to him.

He went as quickly as he could to Pope Urban, presenting the letter to him and narrating many other things that he had seen. In the year of the Lord 1095, the pope, sympathizing with the Holy Land, came into Gaul and conducted a council at Claremont, where he put many good things into effect; at the end he explained the distress of the Holy Land and effectively motivated the faithful to help; he ordered the prelates of the Church to preach the crusade.[21]

Peter also ran about among the princes and the prelates and faithfully promoted the crusade, so that in the year of our Lord 1096 many of the princes and others from France, Spain, England, Germany, Italy, and other parts of the West affixed the cross on their shoulders, intending in one spirit to help the Christians held in servitude. John foreseeing this says: **The seventh angel** That is, Peter the Hermit. **Poured his bowl into the air,** Because by efficacious words he explained the distress of this land to the pope and the princes; for words are formed out of breathed air and are spread through the air as it is held in Book 2 of *De Anima*.[22] **And a loud voice came out of the temple,** That is, from the Church. **From the throne,** That is, from the authority of the highest pontiff. **Saying, "It is done!"** That is, the petition of the Christian people living in Jerusalem was heard.

18. **And there came flashes of lightning, rumblings, peals of thunder,** The rumblings and peals of thunder represent the preaching of the cross, and the flashes represent the signs and marvelous visions that moved many to take up the cross. **And a violent earthquake,** By

many leaving their own lands for this expedition. **Such as had not occurred** Just as it is said in the *Chronicles* of William, never were so many nations gathered in one; the number overwhelmed human calculation, although it was estimated at 600,000.

19. **The great city was split** That is, the army that is called the city as if a unity of citizens; in one spirit they proceeded to Jerusalem. **Into three parts,** For the sake of food and lodging one army followed Peter the Hermit, another people followed the princes who linked with Duke Godfrey, another army left by sea with Bohemond, Duke of Apulia. **And the cities of the nations** That is, of the Saracens. **Fell.** From Nicea in Bithynia and Antioch, which are in the kingdom of Persia, to Jerusalem and beyond to the river of Egypt, cities were held subjugated by the army of the infidels, as the bishop of Tyre describes. **Great Babylon** That is, the Saracen sect, which is called Babylon; that is, confused, because it is filled with confusing laws and commands. **Was remembered by God.** To punish it, therefore it is added: **And gave her the wine-cup. . . .**

20. **And every island fled away,** The Saracens living on the islands near the sea-crossing of the Christians fled out of fear. **And no mountains were to be found;** Many fortifications located in the mountains were destroyed by the Christians.

21. **And huge hailstones . . . dropped from heaven** That is, the war could not be borne by the Saracens, by human and by divine power; for many of them were destroyed by the Christians. **Until they cursed** That is, the Saracens. **God** That is, Christ, who is true God. **For the plague of the hail,** Inflicted on them by the

Christians. **So fearful was that plague.** They were not able to sustain it, as the bishop of Tyre, noted earlier, writes at greater length.

Notes

1. Constantine V (740–75). It is hard for Nicholas to label an emperor wicked, but iconoclasm, as a christological heresy, was not easy for him to gloss over; nor were Constantine's harsh policies against monks and monasticism in general. See Ostrogorsky, *History of the Byzantine State*, pp. 173–75.

2. MGH. SS. 6:333–34. Nicholas frequently cites Sigebert in chapter 16; this pro-imperial chronicler was dear to his heart.

3. Leo IV died prematurely which brought his son Constantine VI to the throne at age ten. Empress Irene became co-emperor with him. See Ostrogorsky, *History of the Byzantine State*, pp. 177–78.

4. This is probably the adoptionist heresy of Felix of Urgel in Spain (d. 818), who was condemned at a synod in Rome during Leo III's papacy. See also Peter, 522.

5. What happened to the pope is repeated here.

6. It seems that an attempt was made to gouge out his eyes and cut his tongue, but it was not successful.

7. Omitted a repetitious section.

8. Charlemagne became emperor in the year 800 and died in 814. Peter and Alexander cite different dates.

9. See Alexander, p. 332 and Peter, p. 521.

10. MGH. SS. 6:336.

11. See chapter 13:11.

12. This thirteenth-century Cistercian chronicler may or may not be the same Cistercian, Hélinand of Froidmont, who also wrote a commentary on the Apocalypse.

13. Nicholas believes the medieval legend that Charlemagne had gone on a crusade to the Holy Land. See Steven Runciman, "Charlemagne and Palestine," *English Historical Review* 1 (1935): 606ff.

14. Nicholas's celebration of Charlemagne is an indication of his general perspective throughout the Commentary as a Francophile. He was very close to the Valois line, which came to power in 1328, and it had an effect on his views. See Philippe Buc, "Pouvoir Royal et Commentaires de la Bible (1150–1350)," *Annales: économies, sociétés, civilizations* 44, no. 3 (Mai–Juin 1989): 705.

15. By 634 the great conqueror Omar had led the Arabs into the Empire, and they swept away the land recently won back for the Persians in short order. Palestine offered more resistance but also fell to Omar.

16. William of Tyre, *Historia rerum in Partibus Transmarinis Gestarum*, PL 201. William of Tyre, the greatest historian of the Crusades, was born in the Holy Land, and after his education and return to Jerusalem he became archbishop of Tyre. His *History of the Deeds Done beyond the Sea* is translated by E. A. Babcock and A. C. Krey (New York: Columbia University Press, 1943).

17. See previous note for William of Tyre. There is no modern critical edition of James of Vitry's *Historia Orientalis*. I have used the Douai, 1597, edition to verify Nicholas's citations.

18. Here Nicholas indicates that he is actually comparing histories and chronicles with one another to examine his exemplars.

19. The Latin word he uses is *peregrationem*. Alexander (p. 354) and Peter (pp. 526, 527) both identify this angel with Alexius.

20. Peter probably did not make it to Jerusalem.

21. *Negotium Crucis* is the term he uses here for the crusade.

22. *De Anima*, Book 2, Chapter 8 discusses these issues.

Chapter 17
THINGS CURRENT AND FUTURE FOR WHICH NICHOLAS HAS NO WORD; FIRST HE RELATES THE INTERPRETATION OF HIS EXEMPLARS

1. **Then one of the seven . . .** According to those who say that the whole text from here to that place: **When the thousand years are ended,** (around the middle of chapter 20 [20:7]) has been fulfilled in the past, the seventh plague is now described more specifically.[1] First I will present their whole interpretation (*litera*); afterwards I will say what seems to me concerning this.[2]

It is divided in two parts, because first, this plague is described specifically; and second, the new advancement of the Christian religion is described in chapter 20. Concerning the first, this plague is about the Saracens, as is clear from what has been said. The second describes the goodness of the Christians defeating them in the following chapter. First it is described under a certain metaphor that is placed first; second, it is explained, at the place: **The angel said to me** (17:7).

Concerning the first it is said: **Then one of the seven angels who had the seven bowls . . .** As those who hold this opinion say, this designates the Emperor Alexius, who according to them as noted above, is called the seventh angel; but this was rejected in that place.[3] Nor can one say conveniently that this angel designates Peter the Hermit, whom I said above was the seventh angel, because this angel is said here to have taught John. Whence it is added: **Came and said to me, "Come, I will show you the judgement of the great whore . . ."** But Peter the Hermit lived more than nine hundred years after John wrote this book. Therefore, it is better to say that St. James, who earlier was called one of the seven angels holding the bowls, was this angel, who, before John saw that vision, had crossed into glory with the martyr's crown (Acts 12:2), and thus he was able to teach him about divinely ordained future things.[4] **"The judgement of the great whore"** That is, of the Saracen sect, as will be said more extensively later. **"Who is seated on many waters,"** That is, has dominion over many waters, as is explained below.

2. **"With whom the kings of the earth have committed fornication,"** Many kings received the law of Muhammed. **"And with the wine of whose fornication the inhabitants of the earth have become drunk."** The people existing under these kings similarly received the Saracen law filled with unclean things.

3. **So he carried me away in the spirit into a wilderness,** To see the status of the Saracens abandoned by God because of their sins. **In the spirit** This vision was not physical but imaginary and intellectual. **And I saw a woman sitting on a scarlet beast** Here one must understand that the Saracens divided in two parts, as was said above—the Turks are designated by the woman due

to their malice and serpentine cleverness; the Egyptians by the beast, because they are less vigorous in intellect and therefore more bestial. It is said, moreover, that the woman is seated on the beast, for the Turks took Judea and Syria from the Egyptians. **Scarlet** That is, red from the blood of Christians. **That was full of blasphemous names,** The Saracens say that Christ was pure man, and thus they blaspheme him, and similarly they deny that the Virgin Mary was the mother of God.

4. **The woman was clothed in purple** The Turks were most opulent in this and in other precious things. **Holding in her hand a golden cup full of abominations** The Turks led and drew many nations into the uncleanness of their law. **And on her forehead was written a name, a mystery: "Babylon."** By saying this, "Mystery," John shows that he is not speaking of the city Babylon but more concerning the Saracen sect in relation to the Turks. **"Mother of whores and of earth's abominations."** The Turks had drawn the eastern peoples into the error of their sect.

6. **And I saw that the woman was drunk with the blood of the saints** According to number and measure they poured Christian blood. "Inebriated" is said as if it means "extra wine," that is, a measure.[5] The Turks were cruel to the Christians, the Egyptians, and the Saracens, according to the bishop of Tyre.[6]

When I saw her, I was greatly amazed. Regarding the patience of God toward this most wicked sect of Muhammed.

7. **But the angel said to me,** Here he places the explanation of the parable, concerning which the angel first proposes the purpose, saying to John, **"Why are you**

so amazed?" That is, everything will be yielded to the glory of God, and of the elect to whom merit increases as a result of the persecution by evil ones. **"I will tell you the mystery"** That is, the hidden significance. **"Of the woman and of the beast"** That is, of the Kingdom of the Turks and of Egypt. Here he proceeds with the proposition by explaining the parable: first, concerning the kingdom of Egypt designated by the beast saying: **"The beast that you saw was,"** The Egyptians had first occupied the dominion of Jerusalem and Judea and afterwards lost that land to the attacking Turks, as was said above. Therefore it is said that the beast was ruling in Judea. **"And is not,"** Ejected by the Turks. **"And is about to ascend from the bottomless pit"** From Egypt, which is to be interpreted as "the lower world." The power of the Turks having been destroyed, the Egyptians regained Judea and Jerusalem with the help of the Christians, as was said. **"And go to destruction."** The Egyptians were killed by the Christians, and those left were ejected, as the bishops James of Vitry and William of Tyre relate describing the history of the Holy Land. **"And the inhabitants of the earth, whose names have not been written . . ."** That is, the Saracens, who were not predestined but foreknown. For the Saracens marvelled how a king so powerful and great might be defeated by a Christian people coming from strange regions and so far away.

9. **"This calls for a mind"** That is, understanding. **"That has wisdom:"** That is, with respect to understanding the secrets of the Scriptures. **"The seven heads are seven mountains"** That is, provinces. **"On which the woman is seated;"** The kingdom of the Turks had

prevailed over Egypt. **"Also they are seven kings,"** That is, princes of these provinces.

10. **"Of whom five have fallen,"** From the dominion of Egypt subjugated to the dominion of the Turks. **"One is living,"** Namely, ruling in Judea and Syria; this is the king of the Turks, who is called the sixth head of the beast. **"And the other"** That is, the king of Egypt, who is called the seventh head. **"Has not yet come;"** To recapture Judea from the hands of the Turks. **"And when he comes,"** The Turks having been defeated. **"He must remain only a little while."** Having taken Jerusalem from the Turks, the king of Egypt was able to hold it only for one year, as the historiographers noted above say.[7]

11. **"As for the beast that was and is not,"** That is, the king of Egypt, as was explained. **"It is an eighth"** With the seven heads mentioned earlier. **"But belongs to the seven,"** That is, from the seven heads. For the seventh head is, as was said, counted twice, because Jerusalem was obtained twice, just as in the preceding chapter Charlemagne is called the fifth angel because of the kingdom of the Franks and the sixth because of his adept rule.[8] **"And it goes to destruction."** Many had been destroyed by the Christians, as the bishops noted above say.

12. **"And the ten horns that you saw are ten kings"** That is, the princes under the king of Egypt, as was said. **"Who have not yet received a kingdom, but they are to receive authority as kings"** This he says because they were not simply kings but also leaders of the battle lines of the army of the king of Egypt. **"For one hour,"** That is, at that time for which it was ordained for that army. **"After the beast."** That is, under the king of Egypt, who is called the beast, as was said, and with the word "after"

he does not refer here to the order of time, but of subjugation.

13. **"These are united"** To fight against the Christians for the king of Egypt; therefore it is added. **"In yielding their power;"** By offering it to the king of Egypt.

14. **"They will make war on the Lamb,"** On his members, namely, Godfrey of Bouillon and the other princes and Christian soldiers. **"And the Lamb will conquer them,"** The Egyptians were frequently defeated by the Christians. **"For he is Lord of lords"** Thus no power is able to resist him. **"And those with him"** Those who are steadfast through faith formed by love until death. **"Are called and chosen"** To glory. **"And faithful."** In the present by grace.

15. **And he said to me,** Here he explains the parable specifically in relation to the kingdom of the Turks. **"The waters that you saw . . . ,"** That is, the kingdom of the Turks as was said above. **"Are peoples and nations and languages."** The kingdom of the Turks subjected to itself Syria, Judea, and most of the eastern peoples.

16. **"And the ten horns that you saw on the beast,"** That is, the ten leaders of the army of the king of Egypt, as was said. **"They and the beast will hate the whore;"** That is, the kingdom of Turks, because between the Egyptians and the Turks there was hatred, first because of the dissension in their superstitions about the law; second because the Turks took Syria and Judea from the Egyptians. **"They will make her desolate and naked;"** First, by means of the Christians to whom, enduring a siege at Antioch, the Egyptian caliph sent greetings and gifts, because they were fighting his adversaries. Thus he comforted the army of the Christians against the Turks, as

is written in the *Historia Hierosolymitana*.[9] Second, through the same because the Turks, having been defeated in parts of Antioch, the Egyptians expelled them from Jerusalem and from Judea, as has been said. **"They will devour her flesh"** This is spoken metaphorically, just as it is said concerning the usurer that he eats him whose goods he snatches through usury. **"And burn her up with fire."** They burned some Turks and the fortifications in which they lived at the same time.

17. **"For God has put it into their hearts to carry out his purpose"** Although God is not the author of wicked sin, God is, nevertheless, the author of the punishment of evil, and thus God punished the Turks through the Egyptians. **"To give their kingdom to the beast,"** That is, to restore the kingdom of Judea to the king of Egypt, which he had possessed for many years before the Turks. **"Until the words of God will be fulfilled."** Concerning the restoration of the Holy Land by the Christian army, as has been said, which was done in a year, as it were, after the Egyptians had expelled the Turks from thence.

18. **"The woman you saw is the great city"** That is, the great number of the Turks. **"That rules over the kings of the earth."** It subjected many kings to itself in the eastern regions, as was said before.

Notes

1. He is alluding to the commentaries of his primary models Peter Auriol and Alexander Minorita, whose interpretations he has followed or criticized all along, but now he will depart from them entirely after recording their interpretations. Consequently, the next three and a half

chapters, with the exception of some interspersed comments, are not those that Lyra himself supports. His commentary will pick up again at 20:7. This strategy has confused the reception of Nicholas's commentary, because many readers in his tradition misunderstood his intent. See my article, "Many Readers but Few Followers."

2. This comment is probably a later addition to Lyra's Commentary, demonstrating that he may have changed his mind about the interpretation of the later chapters of the book. Although he has disagreed with his models throughout, it seems awkward that he would write that with which he disagrees for three and a half chapters and then critique it. More than likely, he re-edited the whole Commentary in 1329, having changed his mind about a number of issues, especially regarding current events.

3. See the previous chapter (16:17) and note.

4. This is another example in which Lyra corrects his own commentary, indicating that he edited his earlier work but sometimes left earlier material in. One suspects he was editing earlier lectures on the text for the *Literal Postill.* These corrections made the Commentary difficult to check for the meaning of one or two verses as is often done with commentaries, and some of his readers misread him as a result. By reading the seventh angel as James, Nicholas is using his principle of contemporaries.

5. This word-play does not work in English: *Ebria* meaning *extra briam.*

6. William of Tyre, *Historia rerum in partibus transmarinis gestarum,* 51, 1 (*PL* 201).

7. It was the use of the word *historiographer* that first made me realize that not only was Nicholas questioning his models philologically, grammatically, textually, and contextually—all of which one would expect in a literal commentary—but he was also using evidence in historical sources to criticize the conclusions of his models. Sometimes he draws different conclusions from the same texts they used,

and sometimes he uses other historians of an event such as the First Crusade. See my article, "Nicholas of Lyra."

8. See note above on Lyra as a Francophile.

9. Ekkehard of Aura († ca. 1126). See also August C. Krey, *The First Crusade: The Accounts of Eye-witnesses and Participants* (Princeton: Princeton University Press, 1921).

Chapter 18
THE INTERPRETATION OF HIS EXEMPLARS CONTINUED

1. **After this I saw** Having described the vileness of the Saracens under the metaphor of the whore and of the beast, here the goodness of the Christians is described under an angelic similitude, first in relation to ecclesiastical persons; and second in relation to lay princes, at the place: **Then a mighty angel took up a stone** (18:21). The first is in two parts according to two notable persons; the second at the place: **Then I heard another voice** (18:4).

Concerning the first it is said, **After this I saw another angel** That is, Bishop Adhemar of Puy, a man of angelic elegance who in the army of the western princes and of other Christians accepted the office of commander to direct the Christian army. **Coming down from heaven,** Proceeding from the loftiness of the papal authority. **Having great authority;** Especially in spiritual things, just as if he was the legate sent from the Lateran. **And the earth** That is, the Christian army. **Was made bright with his splendor.** That is, on account of his life and doctrine.

2. **He called out with a mighty voice,** Preaching in word and in deed. **"Fallen, fallen, is Babylon the great!"**

That is, the Saracen nation, and he says, **"Fallen"** twice, because first the Turks had been destroyed by the Christians; afterwards the Egyptians, as is reported in the history frequently noted earlier; this bishop officially promised the Christians that the Saracens would fall if they would fight valiantly trusting in the help of God.

"It has become a dwelling place of demons," In relation to those put to rout, who saw the wrath of God; nevertheless, they remained obstinant in their infidelity, and thus were possessed more by demons than before; the demons are designated by the birds and the unclean spirits. The reason for this punishment is added:

3. **"For all the nations have drunk of the wine of the wrath"** That is, many, which is a hyperbole to designate the great multitude of the nations infected by the perfidy of Muhammad and meeting the wrath of God.

"And the kings of the earth have committed fornication with her," Many kings accepted this treachery, and similarly many who for temporal gain frequented the land of the Saracens were corrupted. I have heard from a worthy brother that he had seen ships filled with Christian boys whom merchants bought from their poor parents to sell to the sultan at great price. He raised them in the law of Muhammed, because they as yet knew nothing of Christianity, to fight against the Christians as adults; therefore it is added: **"And the merchants of the earth"** It is clear from the text above.

4. **Then I heard another voice** This concerns the second ecclesial person of note, whose holy admonition comes first; second, the beating of the Saracen nation, at the place: **"Render to her . . ."** (18:6); and third, the lamentation of those beaten, at the place: **"Will weep"** (18:9).

Concerning the first, one should know that in the Christian army there was, among others, a certain priest to whom God revealed that many in the army had sinned with Saracen women, on account of which many with God's permission had fallen into the hands of the Saracens, and many more would have fallen had they not repented as a result of the exhortation of this priest.[1] And this is what John says: **Then I heard another voice from heaven,** This revelation came from heaven. **"Come out from her,"** That is, from the filthiness of the Saracens.

5. **"For her sins are heaped high as heaven,"** That is, to be punished before God. **"And God has remembered her iniquities."** In God nothing falls into oblivion, nor is it literally recorded, but the sins are said to be recorded metaphorically when God punishes. . . .

6. **"Render to her . . ."** Here the beating of the Saracens is described because the Christians afflicted them as much and more than they had been afflicted by them. . . .

7. **"Since in her heart she says,"** The Saracen nation, by being haughty concerning their power. **"'I rule as a queen';"** Over other people and especially over Christians. . . .[2]

21. **Then a mighty angel took up** Here the worth of the Christians is described in relation to the lay princes, first, at the time of the first king, Godfrey; and second, at the time of Baldwin, who succeeded him in the following chapter.

The first is divided in two parts, because first the Christian victory is described; and second a rising on account of the joy in the beginning of the following chapter. . . . Concerning the first, it should be known that with Jerusalem having been captured by the Christians, the Saracens having been killed there for the most part, and the others having been ejected, the princes and the army of the Christians instituted Godfrey, duke of Lower Lorraine, as king to protect the regained and acquired land. Then the sultan of Egypt came with a great army to fight the instituted king, who confronted him with a much smaller army, since many Christians had returned home. After eight thousand of the pagans fell, he forced them to flee, and up to two thousand drowned in the port of Ascalon; many among the wicked also perished fleeing into the sea, whose number is unknown. This is what is said: **Then a mighty angel took up a stone** That is, Godfrey, the first king. **Like a great millstone** That is, a strong and constant army. **And threw it into the sea,** Into the army of the Saracens, which is called the sea here because he came through the sea and because there was a great multitude of people there, which is called a sea in which there is much water, as was said in a preceding chapter **"The many waters are many peoples. . ."**[3] (17:15).

Notes

1. Source unknown.

2. From here to verse 18:21 Nicholas is repetitious, and the section is therefore omitted in this translation.

3. The balance of chapter 18 repeats earlier themes.

Chapter 19
THE REPORTING OF NICHOLAS'S EXEMPLARS
CONTINUED

1. **After this I heard** Having described the victory of the Christians, here he describes the rejoicing of the universal Church, and it is divided in two parts: first, he describes the exaltation; second, John's giving thanks, at the place: **And he said to me,** (19:9). Concerning the first he says: **After this I heard what seemed to be a loud voice** That is, the giving of thanks. **In heaven** Of the Church militant regarding so great a destruction of the Saracens and the raising up of the Christians, and also in heaven—in the Church triumphant in which the saints rejoice and give thanks to God for the benefits conferred on the faithful on earth. **Saying, "Hallelujah!"** There are two words in the Hebrew for "Hallelujah," which is equivalent to "Praise:" **"lu"** the name and **"jah!"** Of the Lord. **"Salvation and glory"** For the noted victory must be attributed to God.

2. **"For his judgements are true and just;"** A double reason is added: first, when he says: **"He has judged the great whore"** That is, the Saracen people, specifically in relation to the punishments of the Turks, as was said above in chapter 17. **"Who corrupted the earth with her fornication,"** Because the perfidy of Muhammad killed many people, and, consequently, the second reason is given, when he says: **"And he has avenged on her the blood of her servants."** Of those killed by the Turks and the Egyptians.

3. **Once more they said, "Hallelujah!"** First, for the destruction of the Turks; second, for that of the Egyptians.

Or otherwise, first, for the conquest of the Saracens; second, for the recuperation of the Holy City. **"The smoke"** Namely, of the Saracens. **"Goes up from her forever and ever."** For those killed descended to the fire of Gehenna.

4. **And the twenty-four elders** That is, the cathedrals of the universal Church. **And the four living creatures fell down** That is, the four patriarchates of the Church with their prelates, as was said above in chapter 4. **And worshipped God** For having conferred so great a blessing on the Christians.

5. **And from the throne came a voice** That is, from the apostolic see. **Saying,** By encouraging all Christians to praise God for such great benefits with the certain knowledge of the report.

6. **Then I heard what seemed to be the voice of a great multitude,** That is, of the patriarch in Jerusalem. **Like the sound of many waters** That is, of many people rejoicing, just as was said above in chapter 17:15: **"The many waters are many peoples."** And like the sound of mighty thunderpeals . . . , That is, of the preachers inducing them to praise God. **"For the Lord our God the Almighty reigns . . ."** Namely, the Lord Jesus Christ, who can be said to have ruled in the Holy Land then. When the Saracens had been conquered, the Christians served him there freely.

7. **"Let us rejoice"** In our minds. **"And exult"** Externally, for to exult means as if to dance on the outside, which occurs when the joy of the heart manifests itself externally by sensible signs. **"For the marriage of the Lamb has come . . ."** Thus he shows the love of the Church conferred on parts of Jerusalem, just as a husband

having been reconciled to his wife. **"And his bride has made herself ready;"** To serve her beloved.

8. **"To her it has been granted"** By God. **"To be clothed with fine bright linen . . ."** Through internal holiness and external character, as is clear in what follows: **For the fine linen is the righteous deeds of the saints.** The text is clear.

9. **And he said to me,** Here the thanks given by John is added: first, on account of what is promised, when he says, **And he said to me,** Namely, the angel revealing the mysteries to John, the Divine. **"Write:"** For future remembrance. **"Blessed are those who are invited to the marriage supper of the Lamb."** That is, to the comprehension of the sacrament of the eucharist through faith formed by love. **"These are the true words of God."** Whose messenger was the angel speaking to John and because from God nothing false is possible to proceed.

10. **Then I fell down at his feet** Namely, to give reverence to the angel speaking, which the angel, nevertheless, refused. After the incarnation of the Son of God through which the human nature was assumed by the substance of the Word, the angels avoided being venerated by human nature, which they considered elevated above themselves in the Son of God, who is of the same nature ranked with the Father. **"Worship God!"** By the adoration of worship. **"For the testimony of Jesus is the spirit of prophecy."** That is, all the prophets witness to Jesus Christ.

11. **Then I saw heaven opened,** Here he describes the victory of the Christians at the time of the second king, Baldwin, who succeeded his brother Godfrey in the year 1100. First, his condition is described; second, his notable victory, at the place: **And I saw an angel** (19:17).

Concerning the first, he says: **Then I saw heaven opened,** Because what was hidden in the foreknowledge of God was revealed to John from heaven. **And there was a white horse!** That is, the kingdom of Jerusalem made white by the beauty of holiness, as was said before. **Its rider** Namely, Baldwin having been made king. **Is called Faithful and True,** Literally, he was faithful in deeds and true in words. **And in righteousness he judges** The people subject to him. **And makes war.** Immediately after he was made king, he began to expand his kingdom, notably by driving out the Saracens.

12. **His eyes are like a flame of fire,** His countenance was frightening to the Saracens. **And on his head are many diadems;** In the land of the Philistines, in Tyre, and Sidon, he took many cities in which there were ancient kings. **And he has a name inscribed that no one knows but himself.** He hid his good works, insofar as he was able, from human praise.

13. **He is clothed in a robe dipped in blood,** Namely, of the Saracens killed by him. **And his name is called The Word of God.** For the sake of the honor of the Word of God, he left his native land and went beyond the sea.

14. **And the armies of heaven,** That is, the Templars and the Hospitalers, whose orders had been instituted to fight against the adversaries of the Church, as the expositors have said.[1] **Were following him** In battle. **On white horses** That is, in bodies made white by chastity, because they make a vow of chastity in their profession. **Wearing fine linen.** Through internal and external cleanliness, as was said above.

15. **From his mouth comes a sharp sword** With efficacious words he exhorted and incited his soldiers against

the infidel peoples. **And he will rule them with a rod of iron;** By frequently breaking the pride of the peoples. **He will tread the wine press** . . . Because he was the executor of justice in the shedding of Saracen blood.

16. **On his robe and on his thigh he has a name inscribed, "King of kings and Lord of Lords."** On account of what has been said before, it is clear that he had the quality of a king, especially excellence, on account of which he says, **"King of kings"** according to his circumstances, in that manner by which the rose is called the "flower of flowers."

17. **Then I saw** After having described the famous situation of King Baldwin, he describes a certain notable victory. To understand this one should know that in the fifth year of Baldwin's reign, the princes of Egypt said to their caliph that the time was right to regain the land occupied by the Christians—both because many of the Christian princes had returned to their homelands and because many who remained had been beaten down and impoverished by frequent battles, as the bishop of Tyre says in chapter 3.[2] Some expositors also add that they were excited to this by certain false prophets of the Saracens, who were claiming in short that the rock of the holy sepulchre should be ground into pieces, that the holy cross be submerged into the depth of the sea, and that Christianity be completely blotted out from their lands. Assenting to these things, this caliph prepared a large army throughout the land and sea to obtain what had been suggested to him. After hearing this, the few Christians living there were terrified, but the patriarch of Jerusalem, comforting them, promised them that, if they trusted in God, the victory would be so great that the birds of the air

would eat their fill from the flesh of the Saracens, and he presented the wood of the Lord's cross as an ensign.[3]

Therefore, our own proceeding with great spirit, with five hundred horsemen and two thousand foot soldiers against the enemy of fifteen thousand who had come from their army, overthrew a great multitude of the enemy and turned the rest to flight, retaining a great part of our army. Therefore, John says: **Then I saw an angel** That is, the patriarch of Jerusalem. **Standing in the sun,** Through the eminence of his life and doctrine, as it is written in Ecclus 50:7, "Like the sun shining on the temple of the Most High." **And with a loud voice** By the noted exhortation. **He called to all the birds . . .** It happened that as a result of the fight at his exhortation, the birds ate to their fill.

19. **Then I saw the beast** That is, the sultan of Egypt. **And the kings of the earth** Those subject to him. **With their armies gathered** On sea and on land. **To make war against the rider** That is, with King Baldwin and his army.

20. **And the beast was captured,** That is, the king of Egypt and the false prophets who were caught in their cunning, because the opposite of what they thought happened. **Who had performed in its presence the signs** False ones. **By which he deceived those who had received the mark of the beast** That is, the arms and the standards of the sect of Muhammad. **And those who worshipped its image.** That is, the caliph of Egypt who represented the person of Muhammad. **These two were thrown alive** Namely, the caliph and the prophets, who were not in the battle, and here the singular is used for the plural, namely, "prophet" for "prophets," just as in Ex 8:24, "A great 'fly' came." That is, "Swarms of flies."

Into the lake of fire that burns with sulfur. Because those who remained unfaithful descended into the fire of Gehenna.

21. **And the rest were killed by the sword** Evidently those who went out to fight King Baldwin, as is clear from this text.

Notes

1. In this whole section it must be noted from chapters 17–20 that Nicholas is recording what his models, Peter and Alexander, had said.

2. Book 51, Chapter 3.

3. See Peter, p. 538.

Chapter 20
THE END OF THE INTERPRETATION OF HIS EXEMPLARS AND THE BEGINNING OF NICHOLAS'S RESPONSE

20:1 **Then I saw** Having described the seven plagues in general and specifically, here he describes the new advancement of the Church, and it is divided into two parts: first, he describes this advancement; and second, the renewed persecution of the Christians, at the place: **Then I saw thrones,** (20:4). One should know that some explain the first [part]¹ and the second, in part, with Pope Calixtus and Emperor Henry V, who, with the pope pressuring him under the threat of anathema, renounced the custom that the emperors had used for more than three hundred years of investing bishops and abbots with the staff and ring. The *Chronicle* of Sigebert records that this was done from the time of Charlemagne, to whom the power was conceded by Pope Adrian in a council held at Rome; thus they explain this text.[2]

Then I saw an angel That is, Pope Calixtus. **Holding in his hand the key to the bottomless pit** That is, the power of excommunicating, by which someone is segregated from the fellowship of the faithful. **And a great chain.** That is, the multitude of the cardinals and the prelates assisting him in this deed.

2. **He seized the dragon,** That is, the Roman emperor. **And bound him** Through ecclesiastical censure, lest, in a manner of speaking, he would usurp more ecclesiastical jurisdiction for himself. **For a thousand years,** That is, through the time of Christ, which runs up to the time of Antichrist, and he uses a determinate number for an indeterminate one—just as the twenty-four elders designate all the bishops in chapter 4.

3. **And sealed it over him,** He restrained him under the punishment of excommunication, lest he admit himself into the jurisdiction of the Church, therefore it is added:

4. **Then I saw thrones,** That is, the distinct jurisdictions of the highest emperor and pontiff. **And those seated on them** One exercising the ecclesiastical jurisdiction, the other the temporal. But the subsequent text in the same verse does not agree with this interpretation. **And I also saw the souls of those who had been beheaded** Which some expound as referring to the persecution of Saladin in which many Christians were killed. Similarly, concerning Satan's having been bound for a thousand years, it is said here: **"That he must be let out for a little while."** (20:3). This they explain with regards to the time of Antichrist when the power of the

---

End of the Interpretation; Nicholas's Response 211

devil will be released to deceive the nations. Therefore, to understand the Roman Emperor in what is said of Satan seems to be contradictory and consequently a rather forced exposition.

If one were to interpret this text as if it were fulfilled in the past (I submit myself to better judgement), it seems that it would be better to interpret this text with Pope Innocent III, who approved the orders of the Friars Minor and the Preachers through whom the teaching and preaching of the Church were in a certain way renewed,[3] and the power of the Devil was restricted, whence many illusions of the demons that occurred earlier ceased.

And this is what John says, **Then I saw an angel** (20:1) That is, Pope Innocent III. **Coming down from heaven,** That is, stooping down from the papal summit for Saints Francis and Dominic. **Holding in his hand the key to the bottomless pit** That is, the power to approve these orders to repress the power of the Devil. **And a great chain.** That is, the multiplication of the brothers and of each order.

He seized the dragon, (20:2) Because through their life and teaching the power of the Devil was curbed and will be restrained until the times of the Antichrist; therefore, it is added: **And bound him for a thousand years,** Because then his power will be loosed; therefore, it is added: **After that he must be let out for a little while.** (20:3) For the persecution of Antichrist will be short in comparison to the previous persecutions, namely, of the Jews, of the tyrants, of the heretics, and of the Saracens.[4] **Then I saw thrones,** (20:4) Here he places the renewed persecution of the Christians, which some say refers to the persecution of Saladin, as was said, but to me it seems to refer better to the Tartars who, in the year 1202 having left their land, killed many peoples both Christian and pagan; and thus it is said: **Then I saw thrones,** That is, the metropolitan cities of many kingdoms. **And those seated upon them** That is, the Tartars by subjecting them to themselves. **Were given authority to judge.** That is, the power of killing persons according to the wickedness of that time. **I also saw the souls of those who had been beheaded** This is said in relation to the Christians who were killed confessing the name of Jesus and who totally denied Muhammed, who is said to be the one on the beast—his law, customs, and worship. **They came to life** The life of glory for the souls.

5. **The rest of the dead** Referring to the pagans and infidels killed by the Tartars. **Did not come to life** The life of glory. Those who had died were among the souls in the death of Gehenna. **Until the thousand years were ended.** That is, the time of Christ; for they will rise with others at the end of the world to be punished simultaneously in body and spirit. **This is the first resurrection.** This refers to that which is said concerning the Christians: **They came to life** Supply the life of glory for their souls, which glorious life is called the first resurrection. Indeed the second will be when they will rise in glorious bodies. Because these have salvation that they already possess in their souls and afterwards they will have this bodily; therefore, it is added:

6. **Over these the second death has no power,** That is, the punishment of Gehenna. **But they will be priests of God and of Christ . . .** That is, worshipping him with perfect love. **And they will reign with him a thousand years.** That is, to the general resurrection, and thus it is

---

End of the Interpretation; Nicholas's Response 213

clear that the glory the saints will have before the day of judgement is addressed.

Nicholas's Critique

Therefore it is clear how it is possible to explain this text—from chapter 17 to this place (20:6)—as already completed. Nevertheless, this exposition seems incorrect in many things and forced: first, because it was said in chapter 17 that the beast with seven horns is to be understood as the king of Egypt and the woman of fornication as the king of Turkey, and, afterwards, it was said that one of the seven heads, namely, the sixth, was the king of Turkey. This contradicts what preceded, especially, since the king of Egypt and the king of Turkey were enemies with one another, as it was said in that chapter and earlier.

Similarly, in chapter 18, where the punishment of the Saracen sect is treated under the name, Babylon, many things are discussed such that its total destruction would seem to be understood, when it says: **"Fallen, fallen, is Babylon the great! It has become the dwelling place of demons . . ."** (18:2). Similarly, on account of this it is added afterwards: **"Therefore her plagues will come in a single day—pestilence and mourning and famine— and she will be burned with fire"** (18:8). Similarly, on account of what follows in the same chapter: **"With such great violence Babylon the great city will be thrown down, and will be found no more;"** (18:21). On account of which its total destruction seems to be understood in the previous exposition.

Nevertheless, the Saracens remained in the kingdoms of Egypt and Turkey, which at that time were not acquired by the Christians, nor afterwards, but only one part of Syria and Judea. The Christians lost these places for the most part at the time of Saladin, although after seventy years they were occupied by the Christians; afterwards those which remained Christian, namely, Acre, Tripoli, and certain others, were partly destroyed by the Saracens and partly held.

Similarly, afterwards parts of the nineteenth chapter are interpreted with regards to King Baldwin **On his head are many diadems;** (19:12) On account of the regal cities he acquired. But this seems improbable because his kingdom never grew but remained rather small. Similarly, because it is added there: **He has a name inscribed that no one knows but himself.** (19:12) Because the name of this king and his conditions were known by others; furthermore, the concealment of such a name seems appropriate only for a divine person. (Mt 11:27), "No one knows the Son except the Father, and no one knows the Father except the Son."

Therefore, this text seems to refer not to King Baldwin but to Christ, whence it is added there: **And his name is called The Word of God** (19:13) This name is only appropriate for the Son of God, as is clear in John (1:14), "And the Word became flesh. . . ."

Similarly, because afterwards it is added: **On his robe and on his thigh he has the name inscribed, "King of kings and Lord of Lords."** (19:16). This is explained according to the literal sense by Christ by the saints and catholic doctors.[5]

Similarly, that which is inserted in the same place: **And the armies of heaven . . . were following him . . .** (19:14), is interpreted with the Templars and Hospitalers, but this does not seem well said. That notable victory which is described there was in the fifth year of Baldwin's reign, as was said above. He began to rule in the year A.D. 1100. The order of the Templars, moreover, was approved in the year 1128, and by the example of the Templars the Hospitalers began to take up arms, although they had been instituted before them, as James of Vitry says in chapter 65. Thus it does not appear that they were in the army of this King Baldwin, who only ruled for twenty-eight years, as the same bishop [James of Vitry] says in chapter 93.[6]

Moreover, according to this exposition, everything written in these three chapters of this book since two hundred years and more has been completed, as is clear from the above, and the text immediately following is explained by all to refer to the Antichrist. But that John writes nothing about the status of the Church with so much history left, (since as yet the coming of the Antichrist does not appear near) does not seem appropriate (*conveniens*), especially since it is said commonly by the doctors that in this book John writes the notable things which come to pass for the Church to the end of the world.[7]

On account of these and many other things that could be said against this exposition, it seems (I submit myself to better judgement) that the whole text from the beginning of chapter 17 to this place is not yet fulfilled. And "Because 'I am not a prophet, or the son of a prophet' (Am 7:14), I will not say anything about the future, except what can be taken from Scripture or the words of the saints and established teachers. Therefore, I leave the interpretation of this text to the wise. If the Lord were to grant me its understanding, I would be glad to share it with others."[8]

7. **When the thousand years are ended,** Here the persecution of Antichrist is described concerning which

Scripture and the saints speak in many places, as it is said: **When the thousand years are ended,** That is, the time of the Church to the time of the Antichrist. **Satan will be released** Whose power was restrained by Christ's preaching and his passion and by the apostles' teaching and that of the saintly preachers, which will be slackened at the time of Antichrist; therefore, it is added:

8. **And he will deceive the nations at the four corners of the earth,** Having been seduced by his preachers, some will adhere to Antichrist from all parts of the earth—the devil will cooperate with "lying wonders" (2 Thes 2:9), just as the Gospel of Christ was proclaimed through the apostles, "While the Lord worked with them and confirmed the message by the signs that accompanied it" (Mk 16:20). **Gog and Magog,** By "Gog," which means "roof," Antichrist is understood, who will be the dwelling place of the devil. By "Magog," which means "from the roof," those who follow Antichrist are understood, as has been said more fully in Ez 39. **In order to gather them for battle;** Against the body of the faithful.

9. **They marched over the breadth of the earth** To force everyone to obey Antichrist. Nevertheless, here the future is spoken of using the past tense because of the certitude of the prophecy, which is frequently done in prophecies. **And surrounded the camp of the saints** That is, of the Christians in order to destroy them. **And the beloved city.** That is, Jerusalem, which will be inhabited at that time by Christians, as was said in Ez 39. **And fire came down from heaven** Because Antichrist will be struck by the Archangel Michael, directed by Christ, and a great part of his army will perish with him, as was said in 2 Thes 2.

End of the Interpretation; Nicholas's Response 217

10. **And the devil who had deceived them was thrown into the lake of fire** Because then he will be restrained as before, and his power will be tied up the more in hell. **Where the beast** That is, those living in a bestial fashion. **And the false prophet were,** Of Antichrist, who will deceive them. **And they will be tormented day and night forever and ever.** That is, without end. However, concerning what is said here: **They surrounded . . . the beloved city. And fire came down. . . .** It is clear that John is not speaking here of the Tartars (as some wish to say), because the Tartars did not blockade Jerusalem inhabited by the Christians, nor did fire from heaven devour their army.

11. **And I saw a great white throne** Earlier John described the status of the Church preceding the general judgement, here he describes the judgement itself, saying: **And I saw a great throne** In this the infinite power of the judging Christ is designated. **A white throne** In this the clarity of judgement is indicated, because it will be known to everyone that he is just. **And the one who sat on it;** Namely, Christ, human and God. **The earth and the heaven fled from his presence,** For then they will be changed from the state in which they now exist.

12. **And I saw the dead, great and small,** Because as the Apostle says in 2 Cor 5:10, "For all of us must appear before the judgement seat of Christ." **And books** Supply "of consciences," for all merits and demerits will be known to all so that the justice of the one judging will appear to all. **Also another book was opened, the book of life.** This book is that same book of divine predestination, which is called a book metaphorically because those are represented in it clearly who are simply ordained

to pursue the blessed life, which the book will reveal in the judgement, because then it will appear manifest who are received into blessedness and who not. **And the dead were judged according to their works, as recorded in the books.** Supply "of consciences," because not only will they be judged according to deeds and words, but also according to interior intentions and thoughts.

13. **And the sea gave up the dead** This will happen before the judgement, which precedes the resurrection of the dead, although this is written afterwards, because frequently in sacred Scripture things done earlier are narrated later. Moreover, the dead will rise who have been submerged in both the sea and in an arid place, which is what is meant by "death" here. Even the souls held in hell will return to their bodies, although they are already dead by the death of sin and hell. Therefore it is said here: **Death and Hades gave up the dead. . . .** What was said above is repeated for greater emphasis.

Notes

1. The Antwerp edition uses the word *potestas*, although the sense calls for *partem*, which is the word used in the 1498 Basel edition. It is noteworthy that there is another discrepancy in this section, which is rare for the Lyra editions: *cumminatione*, Antwerp, for *interiectione*, Basel.

2. See Alexander, pp. 408ff. and Peter, pp. 540, 541, who argue that from Charlemagne's time both the emperors and secular authorities were illicitly continuing the custom of investing bishops with the ring and staff or the symbols of their ecclesiastical office. Nicholas will cautiously side with the royal prerogatives.

3. Lyra will not let this interpretation stand but will take it back immediately.

4. This is one of the ways in which Nicholas has outlined the Apocalypse and outlined church history to the twelfth century.

5. Nicholas will now provide a christological interpretation for much of the later portion of the Apocalypse.

6. Nicholas uses both Chapters 65 and 93 of James of Vitry's *Historia Orientalis* to pull the plug from his models' accounts by showing that their interpretations are anchronistic.

7. The sense of this passage is that, if Peter and Alexander and perhaps others interpret chapters 17–20 as completed history and focus primarily on the earlier crusades, then one runs out of chapters in Revelation with too much history left to interpret. The Antichrist is discussed in chapter 20, and Antichrist, for Lyra anyway, was not making an appearance anytime soon. Actually, Peter Auriol had previously raised the issue of the length of the book against the recapitulative method, arguing that there was not enough book for all they wanted to accomplish by reading the Antichrist into every vision of the book. Now Nicholas uses this same argument against Peter's historical linear method, indicating that there has to be room for current events and incomplete history.

8. This important passage reveals much about Nicholas and his critical approach to the texts at hand; it also reveals his sometimes satirical style. For this famous passage, I have used the translation of Bernard McGinn in "Revelation," in *The Literary Guide to the Bible,* ed. Alter and Kermode, p. 534.

Chapter 21
THE CHURCH AFTER THE JUDGEMENT

1. **Then I saw** Having described the final judgement, here John describes the status of the Church after the judgement first in general and then in greater specificity, at the place: **Then one of the seven angels** (21:9). Concerning the first, John predicts the renewal of the sensible world, saying: **Then I saw a new heaven and a new earth;** By these two, the middle elements of fire, water, and air are understood. For all these will be renewed and changed for the better. Therefore, he adds: **For the first heaven and the first earth had passed away,** One should understand not that their substance is changed but that while this remains, they will be improved in their qualities and properties such that in clarity and transparency and similar things they will submit to the glory of the elect, who praise God by created things.

2. **And I** Here John describes the renewal of human nature for the elect, saying: **And I saw the holy city, the new Jerusalem,** That is, the unified society of the elect perfected by charity. **New** In relation to the glory of their bodies. For the bodies of the saints which are corruptible in quality—gross, heavy, and opaque—will rise—immortal, delicate, agile, and transparent. And because this will be done by the glory of the soul being returned to the body, therefore it is said: **Coming down out of heaven** From the highest heaven, so that they may put on their bodies and appear for the judgement. **From God, prepared** With the dowries of soul and body. Therefore it is added: **As a bride.**

3. **And I heard a loud voice** Third, John describes the final consummation. First, in relation to the elect.

Second, in relation to the reprobate, at the place: **"But as for the cowardly,"** (21:8). Concerning the first he says: **And I heard a loud voice** Of divine majesty. **Saying, "See the tabernacle of God is among mortals."** That is, the inseparable dwelling of God with humans, because the blessed will have that power by clear vision and perfect enjoyment. And because by this all the evil of sin and of punishment is excluded, it is added:

4. **"And death will be no more. For the first things have passed away."** In the Church militant, which is called the terrestrial Jerusalem. These things are now and will be until the judgement.

5. **And the one who was seated on the throne said,** Namely, God, three in one. **"See, I am making all things new."** Namely, the heavens, the elements, and the bodies of the elect, as is clear from the above. **Also he said, "Write this,"** To inform the Church.

6. **Then he said to me, "It is done!"** That is, the consummation is the joy of the elect. **"I am the Alpha and the Omega,"** Which is explained with what follows: **"The beginning and the end."** For Alpha is the first letter in Greek and Omega the last. For God is the effective cause from whom all things are produced and the end to which all things are ordered. **"To the thirsty"** That is, in a manner intended for the one desiring. **"I will give water as a gift from the spring of the water of life."** That is, the participation of the blessed life. **"As a gift"** Although those who have grace merit the blessed life condignly; nevertheless, grace itself is given as a gift, "Otherwise grace would no longer be grace" (Rom 11:6).[1]

7. **"Those who conquer"** The flesh, the world, and the devil. **"Will inherit these things."** By an eternal in-

heritance. **"And I will be their God"** Giving glory. **"And they will be my children."** Through perfect assimilation (1 Jn 3:2), "When he is revealed, we will be like him, for we will see him as he is."

8. **"But as for the cowardly,"** Here he treats the final consummation in relation to the reprobate—to those inclining by worldly fear to mortal sins and those persevering in them. **"The faithless,"** That is, to the Jews, the Saracens, and the rest of those rejecting the Catholic faith.[2] **"The polluted,"** That is, those who revert to immoderate sins after their pardon, just as a dog is accustomed to return to its vomit. **"The murderers,"** For instance, having been done by deliberation. **"The fornicators,"** Fornication means all the rest of the carnal vices. **"The sorcerers,"** That is, by sorceries and fortune telling. **"The idolaters,"** Those offering creatures the worship owed to God. **"And all liars,"** Pernicious lying. Other vices are understood here. **"Their place"** That is, retribution. **"Will be in the lake that burns with fire and sulfur."** That is, the punishment of hell, which is called the second death.

9. **Then one of the seven angels . . . came and said to me,** Here the status of the Church after the judgement is described more specifically. One should know, however, that some explain this concerning a time before the judgement, and also before the coming of Antichrist, which they strive to show on account of what is included in the following chapter (22:11): **"Let the evildoer still do evil, and the filthy still be filthy, and the righteous still do right. . . ."** After the judgement there will be no time nor place for merits or demerits. They say, therefore, that this angel introduced here is understood to be Pope

Innocent III, who approved the orders of the Friars Minor and Preachers, who are called here the new city, Jerusalem,[3] according to Prv 18:19: "A brother helped by a brother is like a strong city."[4]

Both orders were instituted for the same work, namely, preaching the Gospel. Therefore, they say that Francis and Dominic, the founders of these orders, are the foundation of this city. Moreover, there are twelve foundations, it is said (21:14), because they are imitators of the twelve apostles; the wall is the regular observance through the precepts and rules; the gates are the religious entering from the four parts of the earth (21:13), because some are entering these orders from all parts of the earth; the angels standing at the gates (21:12) are the ministers and the provincial priors, who by themselves or through others receive those coming to the order.[5] Thus, as they are able, they adapt other words here to their proposition. Although this exposition is able to be preserved in some mystical sense, it is not possible in the literal sense, as I believe.[6]

First, because it is said that the angel who is introduced here teaches John saying: **"Come, I will show you"** (21:9) One cannot say this of Pope Innocent, since he lived more than one thousand years after John.[7] Similarly, because it is said about this city: **I saw no temple in the city,** (21:22) These orders, however, have churches. Similarly, because it is added: **And the city has no need of sun or moon** (21:23) And afterwards: **But nothing unclean will enter it, nor anyone who practices abomination or falsehood. . . .** (21:27) These orders, however, need the illumination of the sun and the moon; neither are all who enter unstained; nor do all who are good when they enter persevere in the good, but many become apostates and the worst of persons. As Augustine says, "Just as I have not found any better than those who live their professions well in monasteries, so also I have found none worse than those who have fallen into sin in monasteries."[8]

On account of these things and many others which can be raised against this interpretation, insofar as they speak of the literal sense, it seems to me that the city described here is the heavenly Jerusalem, whence after the promised words about entrance into the city it is added: **But only those who are written in the Lamb's book of life** (21:27). These are the predestined, who, furthermore, enter the heavenly Jerusalem and no others. As I said before, here the status of the Church triumphant is described in greater specificity. First with reference to the sublime site, and then to the person speaking to John, when it is said: **Then one of the seven angels . . . came** (21:9). This refers to St. James, who above in chapter 17 was called one of the seven angels carrying the bowls, and he preceded St. John into glory; therefore, by the will of God it was possible to reveal to him the secrets of heaven.

9. **"Come, I will show you the bride,"** That is, the heavenly Jerusalem, as was said in the first chapter, which is called the wife of the Lamb, in a special manner, because it is joined to him inseparably and eternally. Thus it is not the Church militant that will cease to exist at the end of the world, but the imperfect at the coming of the perfect and the figure at the arrival of the thing figured. Just as the old law was imperfect and is a figure of the new law, so the Church militant is a figure of the Church triumphant, whose status will be perfect in every way in

the general resurrection. The elect will be separated from the reprobate, and they will be perfectly blessed in body and in soul. They will rise in glorious bodies because the glory of the soul will return to the body.

10. **And in the spirit** This he says to show that he does not see the glory of the elect at that time, as it will be in itself; he sees a representation of it, namely, in the city which is described below, which he saw by an imaginary vision whose significance he understood, otherwise it would not be a prophetic vision, as was presented in the first book of the Psalms and the first book of Daniel.[9]

To a great, high mountain. By this mountain the heavenly Jerusalem is indicated. . . .[10]

14. **And the wall of the city has twelve foundations.** That is, the twelve articles of faith, according to which the Apostle says in Heb 11:1: "Faith is the assurance of things hoped for. . . ." That is, of heavenly goods, which are the things hoped for. And in this definition the assurance of faith is taken as the beginning or the foundation, because the foundation is the beginning of a house. Through formed faith the happiness of heaven begins in us, as is more fully said in Heb 11. **And on them are the twelve names of the twelve apostles of the Lamb.** That is, of Christ. There are twelve articles of faith concerning Christ—six pertaining to his divinity and six to his humanity—according to the more common distinction of the articles, although some distinguish fourteen articles of faith—seven concerning his divinity and seven concerning his humanity. The names of the apostles are said to be written on the foundations because they first published the faith of Christ by preaching and by dying for it. . . .

19. **The first foundation was jasper,** It was said above that these foundations represent the twelve articles of faith. Among the six pertaining to the divinity of Christ, the first concerns the unity of God, which is the foundation for the faithful in removing errors of people about the powers of many gods. Jasper, therefore means that which purges the eyes and sharpens and comforts the vision, as it is said in the book concerning the properties of things. **The second sapphire,** The second article concerns the trinity of persons, a doctrine that increases the mystical body of the Church. Earlier it was in one small people, the Jews; but through this faith in the Trinity, it extended itself to the multitude of the converted peoples. Therefore, it is signified through sapphire, which animates the human body and conserves it as a whole. **The third agate,** The third article concerns the work of creation, which pertains to God alone, and faith in this article protects against the illusions of demons so that they are not adored. Therefore, it is signified through agate which strengthens one against the illusions of demons and conserves the virtues. **The fourth emerald,** The fourth article concerns the work of sanctification through grace, which heals mortal sin and provides sweet words in prayer. Emerald also signifies that which strengthens against epilepsy.

20. **The fifth onyx,** The fifth article concerns the resurrection of bodies—faith in which produces humility and purity, by inferring the corruptibility of the body, which must be kept humble in appearance and activity because the resurrection to glory in the future. **The sixth carnelian,** The sixth article concerns our glorification—faith in which causes joy in the soul and expels fear. Knowing it will be glorified, it does not fear death on

Christ's account but always rejoices (Mt 5:11). "When people revile you and persecute you and utter all kinds of evil against you falsely on my account. Rejoice and be glad, for your reward is great in heaven. . . ."

The seventh chrysolite, The first article pertaining to the humanity of Christ concerns his conception and his birth of a virgin; this faith strengthens the human nature in the conception of Christ by the Word and prevails against the dark fears of the vices, and, because Christ was born in the middle of the night, the angels said to the shepherds, "Fear not!" (Lk 2:10). Therefore it follows: "Glory to God in the highest, and on earth peace to those of good will." **The eighth beryl,** The second article concerns the passion of Christ; that is, his death and burial. This faith makes one conquer the tribulations of this world, "Since therefore Christ suffered in the flesh . . ." (1 Pt 4:1). **The ninth topaz,** the third article about the humanity of Christ pertains to the descent of his soul into hell; this faith avails against the dangers brought by demons, because by his descent they were despoiled and their power was diminished. Therefore it is signified through topaz which is effective against anger; that is, against madness, which is frequently aggravated and increased by angry demons. **The tenth chrysoprase,** The fourth article concerns the resurrection of Christ, which is the cause of our future resurrection, because this faith avails against the corruption through sin of the body and soul. All corruption is lifted in the resurrection of Christ, signified by chrysoprase, which is effective against leprosy. **The eleventh jacinth,** The fifth article concerns the ascension of Christ to heaven—assumed in his humanity—which faith provides vigor to the faithful such that they may follow him as his body. "Seek the things that are above . . ." (Col 3:1). **The twelfth amethyst.** The sixth concerns the coming judgement in which Christ will appear in the form of a glorified humanity; this faith makes an anxious and watchful humanity, so that in that fearful judgement he may render an account concerning thoughts, words, and deeds. . . .

22. **I saw no temple in the city,** Here the heavenly Jerusalem is described in relation to the worship of God. It should be understood that the worship of God at the time of the Old Testament was a figure in contrast to the worship observed at the time of the New Testament. "These things happened to them to serve as an example . . ." (1 Cor 10:11). Indeed, worship in the New Testament is in its own way a figure of worship in heaven, which the Church militant represents as it is able through heavenly proclamations, as it is said in that sequence: "The Church represents the joys of the celestial mother, which representation is in the material temple and through physical worship." The status of the heavenly beatitude is not a figure of anything expected, for God will be seen clearly there—beheld and venerated in actual presence. Therefore, John says, **And I saw no temple there,** Because God is not worshipped there in figures but in God's presence. **For the Lord God the Almighty is its temple, and the Lamb.** The blessed are refreshed interiorly by the vision of the divinity and exteriorly by the vision of the humanity of Christ. Thus they worship and adore each nature insofar as the humanity is joined to the divinity.

23. **And the city has no need of sun or moon to shine on it,** That is, by corporeal light. **For the glory of**

God is its light, Because the elect are perfectly enlightened.

24. **And the nations will walk** That is, the elect. **By its light,** For they do everything by God's light. **And the kings of the earth will bring their glory** A king is one who rules, and, indeed, all things and people are governed and ruled by the holy angels. Therefore, here and in many other places in Scripture, angels are called rulers of the earth, and the elect are led by their governance to beatitude and their glory is increased. According to this, it is said here that the kings of the earth will bring their glory into the heavenly city.

25. **Its gates will never be shut by day**— From the time of the passion of Christ, through which the doors of heaven have been opened, they remain and will remain open. For there the purified souls are received. The time is said, moreover, from the passion—**The day**—Because then the light of glory was given to the holy fathers in limbo, on account of which Christ said to the thief on the cross, "Today, you will be with me in Paradise" (Lk 23:43).

Notes

1. A common medieval citation of Romans to avoid the implication of Pelagianism in the discussion of merits.

2. An important list of those he considers outside salvation.

3. See Alexander, pp. 467ff. for this most interesting interpretation.

4. The Vulgate differs from the NRSV here, and the Hebrew is unclear. Lyra's text is translated here.

5. See Alexander, p. 473, including note 4.

6. In other words, this mystical interpretation could be used in preaching, but it is not the literal sense.

7. Here Nicholas's rule of contemporaries applies.

8. St. Augustine, Letter 78, "To The Church at Hippo" (404) [Probably from Carthage]. It is interesting that Augustine cites Rv 22:11 after the passage which Nicholas quotes. See *St. Augustine's Letters 1–82*, The Fathers of the Church, vol. 12 (Washington, D.C.: Catholic University Press, 1951), p. 384.

9. The "Prologue" of Nicholas's *Commentary on the Psalter* is translated in Minnis and Scott, *Medieval Literary Theory and Criticism*, pp. 271–74.

10. From here to the end of chapter 21 the Commentary is a detailed analysis of the heavenly Jerusalem and an extended christological meditation from which the section on the twelve aspects of Jesus' divinity and humanity has been selected. (21:19–20).

Chapter 22
THE REFRESHMENT OF THE SAINTS

1. **Then the angel showed** Here, finally, the heavenly city Jerusalem is described as a refreshment of its citizens. It is divided in two parts; first, this feast is described and then the activity of those feasting, at the place: **Nothing accursed will be found there. . .** (22:3). Concerning the first one should say that the refreshment of the saints is not understood by us, unless by a corporeal image. Moreover, for refreshment two things are needed, namely, food and drink. First, the drink is described: **And he**

showed me the river of the water of life, Through this the Holy Spirit is understood, whence the savior says in Jn 7:38, "As the Scripture has said, 'Out of the believer's heart shall flow rivers of living water'." The evangelist explains, "Now he said this about the Spirit, which believers in him were to receive" (Jn 7:39). Moreover, the Holy Spirit, to whom goodness and sweetness is attributed, refreshes the saints with a sweet drink signified by the river of the water of life; that is, giving the glory of life. **Proceeding** For the Holy Spirit proceeds from the Father and the Son.

2. **Through the middle of the street of the city.** To refresh the whole host of the blessed. **On either side of the river** Here he describes the heavenly food as refreshment, when he says: **On either side** That is, here and there. **Is the tree of life** That is, Christ, who according to his divinity is everywhere just as the Holy Spirit, since they are one in essence. **With its twelve kinds of fruit,** Which also are called the fruits of the Spirit in Gal 5:22–23. The works of the Trinity are indivisible in the Son and in the Holy Spirit. It should be known that these fruits are possessed one way in life through grace and in another in glory, just as has been said concerning the four cardinal virtues, because of these some are the acts of pilgrims and some of those who possess heavenly glory. The first fruit in Gal 5 is love, which in heaven is to be totally transformed through love into the vision of God; the second is joy, which is to be delighted in the vision of God; the third is peace, which is to be totally at rest in the same; the fourth is patience, which in this life is not to be broken by adversaries—in heaven, where there is no adversity, it is to be firmly established in God; the fifth is

kindness. . . . **Producing its fruit each month;** The Hebrew month begins with the first moon, which is called the new moon; here the continuation is meant, and thus each month means the eternity of this fruit, because it always remains new and endures. In the same way, Isaiah writes in the last chapter: "From new moon to moon, and from sabbath to sabbath, all flesh shall come to worship before me, says the Lord" (Is 66:23). **And the leaves of the tree are for the healing of the nations.** Leaves mean words according to common parlance. Therefore, the leaves of the tree are the words of Christ contained in the Gospel, which are for the healing of the nations. By the preaching of the Gospel the nations throughout the world have been converted to Christ.

3. **Nothing accursed will be found there** Here he describes the activity of those feasting. It should be known that in carnal feasting people are accustomed to lend their tongues to blasphemies and vices; therefore, the tongue of the rich man who feasted sumptuously was tormented in hell (Lk 16:17–24). This, however, will not be present in heaven, since it is said, **Nothing accursed will be found there anymore** (22:3). Only the giving of thanks and praise. **But the throne of God and of the Lamb will be in it,** Their majesty will especially shine there. **And his servants** The holy and blessed angels. **Will worship him;** By doing whatever pleases him.

4. **They will see his face,** Clearly and openly. **And his name will be on their foreheads.** That is, it will be manifest to all, because they are his servants.

5. **And there will be no more night;** This has been explained above; here, however, it is repeated to make it clearer, because to worship God is to rule. Therefore, it

follows: **They will reign forever and ever.** That is, eternally.

6. **And he said to me,** This is the last principal part of this book, placed at the end as an epilogue. First, the book is commended; second a brief recitation of prescriptions, at the place: **"Let the evildoer"** (22:11); and third, a confirmation of the sayings, at the place: **I warn everyone** (22:18). Concerning the first it is said: **And he said to me,** (22:6) That is, the angel. **"These words"** Written by you. **"Are trustworthy and true,"** For they proceeded from the first truth. Therefore it follows: **"For the Lord, the God of the spirits of the prophets,"** Although the Holy Spirit touches the minds of all the prophets; nevertheless, his effects are many and varied in their minds. **"Has sent his angel to show his servants"** Through John. **"What must soon take place."** Because these things have been pre-ordained by God, whose ordaining cannot be frustrated, therefore it follows:

7. **"See, I am coming soon!"** By its fulfillment, the truth of this book appears. Second, its usefulness is addressed, when he says, **"Blessed is the one who keeps. . . ."** Third, his authority as the writer, when he says:

8. **"I, John,"** That is, while living on earth he was more than human—equal to the angels—which is why the angel refused to receive his reverence, which he wished to offer him when it is said: **And when I heard and saw them,** The text is clear. The fourth addresses the understanding of this book, when the angel says:

10. **"Do not seal etc."** That is, do not hide the understanding of the words, because in many places they are sufficiently clear such that by their study the way is opened to understand others to some extent, as I have

described in those places.[1] **"For the time is near."** Of the fulfillment of the Scripture.

11. **"Let the evildoer still do evil,"** As was said above concerning the distinction between the elect and the reprobate. In relation to this he says: **"Let the evildoer"** By sinning against the neighbor. **"Still do evil,"** That is, he will do evil; here the subjunctive is used for the indicative. He speaks about the foreknowledge of the reprobate who die in mortal sin. **"And the filthy"** That is, by sinning against themselves. **"Still be filthy,"** That is, he will be filthy. **"And the righteous"** By living justly towards the neighbor. **"Still do right,"** That is, he will do justice. He is speaking concerning the just who are predestined to die in final grace. **"And the holy still be holy."** By living purely. As was said frequently earlier in relation to the rewards for the good and the reprobate; here he speaks in the person of Christ.

12. **"See, I am coming soon;"** To show that he is able, he says:

13. **"I am the Alpha and the Omega,"** That is, the effective and final cause of all things, just as A is the first letter in Greek and Ω the last.

14. **Blessed are those who wash their robes,** By the waters of penance in the present. Which in some books— in old Bibles—is added. **So that they will have the right to the tree of life** That is, in the future they will enjoy Christ by whose divinity they are fed internally and by his humanity externally. **And may enter the city by the gates.** That is, by keeping the commandments they enter eternal life.

15. **Outside are the dogs,** That is, the gluttons and detractors barking at the good. **And sorcerers,** That is,

filled with the poison of envy. **And fornicators,** That is, killing themselves. **And murderers,** Bodily and spiritually. **And idolaters,** Which is the sin directly against God. **And everyone who loves and practices falsehood.** Who loves to spread lies; for hypocrisy is lying in deed.

16. **"It is I, Jesus, who sent my angel to you"** Namely, the punishment of the wicked and the reward of the good. **"With this testimony for the churches."** Which are throughout the world. Earlier the merits of Christ were frequently noted; here he speaks to them in his person: **"I am the root and the descendent of David,"** That is, from the root of Jesse, just as David is from his line according to his humanity, as it is said in Is 1, "A shoot shall come out from the stump of Jesse, and a blossom shall grow out of his roots." This blossom is Christ according to the literal sense, as has been said more extensively at that place. **"The bright and morning star."** In relation to his divinity showing his coming to every person in this world (Jn 1:8).

17. **The Spirit and the bride say, "Come."** Note this is the true reading, and the correct books have it such; moreover the Holy Spirit addresses Christ. **"Come."** Namely, in judgement to reward the just, which is possible to be understood in two ways. In one way, because he causes the just to say this who desire to be rewarded by Christ in the judgement—in the same manner of speaking, when it is said in Rom 8:26 that "the Spirit intercedes for us with sighs too deep for words"; that is, "he causes to plead," according to all the catholic expositors. In another way, because just as the Son was sent into the world by the Father and the Holy Spirit, as it is said in his person in Is 48:16: "And now the Lord God

has sent me and his spirit" (As has been shown more fully in that place); so in the coming judgement he is sent by the Father and the Spirit. **And the bride** That is, the Church militant which longs to be joined to the Church triumphant, which will occur in the final judgement.

Let everyone who hears From the Spirit through inspiration and from the Church through preaching. **Say, "Come."** That is, by desiring the advent of Christ, whence in Lk 21:28 the Savior says, "Now when these things begin to take place, stand up and raise your heads." That is, "Let your hearts rejoice," as Gregory says, "since your redemption is drawing near."[2] **And let everyone who is thirsty** Desiring glory. **Come.** Through grace. **Let everyone who wishes take the water of life** That is, the glory of the spirit. **As a gift.** For this the person has in baptism by Christ's merit, unless an obstacle is set up.

18. **I warn everyone who hears the words of the prophecy of this book:** This is the last part in which the confirmation of what has been said is set forth, because nothing superfluous or incomplete is contained there; therefore, it is added: **If anyone adds to them,** Namely, contradictions to the truth of Gospel, as the heretics, the Ebionites and Cerinthus, did, who at the time were adding discordance to the truth of the Gospel and were subtracting some things from its truth saying that Christ did not exist before Mary.[3] This, moreover, does not exclude the things that can be said licitly to explain the Holy Scriptures, as the holy doctors do.

20. **The one who testifies to these things says,** Christ. **"Surely I am coming soon."** To judge each one at death; for however someone is found at death, as such will the individual be presented at the judgement. He will

come to judge everyone generally at the general resurrection. **Come, Lord Jesus!** This John says to conform himself to the Holy Spirit and to the Church, and therefore, he adds his prayer for all the faithful:

21. **The grace of the Lord Jesus be with all the saints. Amen.**

Notes

1. This is a principle established by Augustine in *On Christian Doctrine*, that difficult passages in the Bible can often be explained by clear ones.

2. Gregory, Sermon 1, *Sermons on the Gospels* (*PL* 76:1079B).

3. This reference could refer to the fact that some Ebionites were supposed to have rejected the virgin birth.